To, Mike & Monica
Christmas 2014

Jim

RELIGIOUS THOUGHTS

A Historical Perspective

JAMES WATSON

RELIGIOUS THOUGHTS
A HISTORICAL PERSPECTIVE

iUniverse books may be ordered through booksellers or by contacting:

iUniverse LLC
1663 Liberty Drive
Bloomington, IN 47403
www.iuniverse.com
1-800-Authors (1-800-288-4677)

ISBN: 978-1-4917-3759-0 (sc)
ISBN: 978-1-4917-3760-6 (hc)
ISBN: 978-1-4917-3758-3 (e)

Library of Congress Control Number: 2014910690

Printed in the United States of America.

iUniverse rev. date: 06/23/2014

CONTENTS

PREFACE

I realise that a tremendous amount of material has been written on the subject of religion and its apparent connection to violence, especially since the dreadful events of September 11 2001, but my thoughts and concerns go way back beyond that date. Why do these concerns bother me so much? I really don't know. I think if people were honest with themselves, a lot more would admit to having the same questions and concerns I have but for reasons known only to themselves would rather not voice them. I suspect a lot of people would rather just leave their 'blinkers' on so as not to have to deal with niggling doubts even when faced with facts and the evidence that continues to surface. Of course there are those who don't give a rat's ass about anything.

I was brought up 'Methodist', attended Sunday School, Bible Class and Evening Services and belonged to The Christian Endeavour, a youth organization of the time. Then my teens came along and I began to think outside the box. So I drifted away from church and chapel as so many of us did but thoughts and questions on religion just didn't stop because I drifted away. My wife and I were married in the Church of England and our children went to Sunday School from an early age so as to give them the same opportunity of choice when they grew older to understand better.

The more recent years have brought my questions and concerns on religion more into focus and I have given them a higher priority, so much so that I decided to try and put my thoughts on paper and at that point, as I was also concerned with the Middle East problems I began to think of the possibility of a book, combining the two issues. But the more I read, the more I began to realise that the two issues, even though there is some common ground, especially in the early years, cannot be combined without complicating already very complex subjects. So this book will, hopefully, concern itself with religion only.

The basic theme of the book originally was to be solely religion's association with violence and compiling evidence to substantiate my claims but after spending hours reading books and essays on the subject of religion and its undeniable connection with violence and compiling pages of my own it has become very apparent that I am not alone in these discomforting thoughts. So much so and in the shadow of an overwhelming multitude of scholars and learned persons who have written on this subject that I have decided to relinquish my endeavours in this regard and proceed in another direction but the thread of religion and violence throughout the book will be quite obvious.

I had originally intended to compile a list of religious conflicts to be able to say "There, see what happened because of religion" but keeping a scorecard as far as which conflicts were directly a cause of religion and which were not is impractical, in fact attempts to do this have already been made but still leave results open to interpretation and opinion. So my direction now is to try and understand why religion has become so diversified and corrupted to the point that there are so many confusing elements and man-made sects derived from the so-called Abraham original that it is obviously nowhere near what God intended it to be and also to refresh my memory and try to establish, for my own benefit at least, the difficulties facing the early converts especially at the time of the exile. How did the Children of Israel manage to regroup? Did they have or indeed do they have now, any legal rights to the land they called home prior to the exile? History tells us they took that land by force from the original inhabitants. Why did God allow all this grief to happen if he is so powerful and all seeing? To make us stronger? Doubt is an awful thing, but common sense is a greater human blessing.

Please forgive my doubts and my wanderings but I still have faith.

INTRODUCTION

Where to start? The book "Religious Thoughts" is about religion and what may be considered to be, not just its negative and violent impact on the world to date but also to try and understand why there are so many 'religions'. Or are they just derivatives or sects of the original?

The word "religion" covers a multitude of sins so let's find out first what the word actually means and how it was formed.

Noun - religion

1.

   A **set** of beliefs concerning the cause, **nature,** and purpose of the universe, especially when considered as the creation of a superhuman agency or agencies, usually involving devotional and ritual observances, and often containing a moral code governing the conduct of human affairs.

2.

   A specific fundamental set of beliefs and practices generally agreed upon by a number of persons or sects: **the Christian religion; the Buddhist religion.**

3.

   The body of persons adhering to a particular set of beliefs and practices: **a world council of religions**.

4.

   The life or state of a monk, nun, etc.: **to enter religion.**

The practice of **religious** beliefs; ritual observance of faith.

Word Origin & History religion c.1200, "state of life bound by monastic vows," also "conduct indicating a belief in a divine power," from Anglo-Fr. religiun (11c.), from O.Fr. religion "religious community," from L. religionem (nom. religio) "respect for what is sacred, reverence for the gods," in L.L. "monastic life" (5c.); according to Cicero, derived from relegare "go through again, read again," from re- "again" + legere "read" (see **lecture).** However, popular etymology among the later ancients (and many modern writers) connects it with religare "to bind fast" (see **rely),** via notion of "place an obligation on," or "bond between humans and gods." Another possible origin is religiens "careful," opposite of negligens. Meaning "particular system of faith" is recorded from c.1300.

"To hold, therefore, that there is no difference in matters of religion between forms that are unlike each other, and even contrary to each other, most clearly leads in the end to the rejection of all religion in both theory and practice. And this is the same thing as atheism, however it may differ from it in name." [Pope Leo XIII, Immortale Dei, 1885]

Modern sense of "recognition of, obedience to, and worship of a higher, unseen power" is from 1530s. Religious is first recorded early 13c. Transferred sense of "scrupulous, exact" is recorded from 1590s.

So there we have it – that small word "religion" – but what a huge impact it has on life (and death).

Regarding the book itself, hopefully the storyline will evolve as the book progresses on its travels through history and it will be interesting to see how the various "man-made" religions were formed and hopefully why they were formed. Why were the "minor" religions started – for example: Protestant, Methodist, Baptist, Presbyterian etc.

And did these religions coincide with or cause directly or indirectly major military conflicts.

What is disturbing is the fact that the very area where the senior patriarch, Abraham, came from is considered the cradle of civilization, the first written word originated in Uruk in the ancient land of Sumer in Mesopotamia and this same area, now Iraq is where so much trouble is still festering and the civilizations that these countries had and the art and the inventions that all came out of those areas have faded into the past. What has this got to do with religion? Not sure, but maybe it will become clearer.

The fact that there are literally hundreds of "religions" kind of makes one wonder why this is when God supposedly spoke only to Abraham initially and then Moses later on and the three major "religions", Judaism, Christianity and Islam were formed from this. (Christianity obviously later after Jesus Christ) Why has man interfered and formed other "religions"? As in politics, could money be the driving factor?

Just looking at lists and descriptions of religions actually boggles the mind, even only the Christian ones. This in itself kind of infers that the whole aspect of God and religious worship is ridiculously silly and is best put in the bottom drawer along with the socks and underwear.

The following is a partial list of Christian religions just for reference:

Abrahamic Religions are **monotheistic** religions which believe they descend from Abraham.

JUDAISM is the oldest Abrahamic religion, originating in the people of ancient Israel and Judea. Judaism is based primarily on the Torah, a text which some Jews believe was handed down to the people of Israel through the prophet Moses in 1400 BC. This along with the rest of the Hebrew Bible and the Talmud are the central texts of Judaism. The Jewish people were scattered after the destruction of the Temple in Jerusalem in 70 AD. Today there are about 13 million Jews, about 40 per cent living in Israel and 40 per cent in the United States.

CHRISTIANITY is based on the life and teachings of Jesus of Nazareth (1st century) as presented in the New Testament. The Christian faith is essentially faith in Jesus as the Christ, the Son of God, and as Savior and Lord. Almost all Christians believe in the Trinity, which teaches the unity of Father, Son (Jesus Christ), and Holy Spirit as three persons in One Godhead. Most Christians can describe their faith with the Nicene Creed. As the religion of Byzantine Empire in the first millennium and of Western Europe during the time of colonization, Christianity has been propagated throughout the world. The main divisions of Christianity are, according to the number of adherents:

CATHOLIC CHURCH, headed by the Pope in Rome, is a communion of the Western church and 22 Eastern Catholic churches.

There was some thought that Catholicism came later (after the fact, as it were) and is purely a money making business, and so it is, but it turns out that it probably is the one true original church, founded by St Peter on the Rock with the blessing of Jesus Christ and that everything else following is a load of codswallop.

PROTESTANTISM, separated from the Catholic Church in the 16th-century reformation and split into many denominations,

EASTERN CHRISTIANITY which include Eastern Orthodoxy, Oriental Orthodoxy and the Church of the East.

There are other smaller groups, such as Jehovah's Witnesses and The Latter Day Saints Movement whose inclusion in Christianity is sometimes disputed.

ISLAM refers to the religion taught by the Islamic prophet Muhammad, a major political and religious figure of the 7th century AD. Islam is the dominant religion of northern Africa, the Middle East, and South Asia. As with Christianity, there is no single orthodoxy in Islam but a multitude of traditions which are generally categorized as Sunni and Shia, although there are other minor groups as well. Wahhabi is the dominant Muslim schools of thought in the Kingdom of Saudi Arabia. There are also several Islamic republics, including Iran, which is run by a Shia Supreme Leader.

The Bahai Faith was founded in the 19th century in Iran and since then has spread worldwide. It teaches unity of all religious philosophies and accepts all of the prophets of Judaism, Christianity, and Islam as well as additional prophets including its founder Bahaullah.

Smaller regional Abrahamic groups, including Samaratanism (primarily in Israel and the West Bank), the Rastafari Movement (primarily in Jamaica), and Druze (primarily in Syria and Lebanon).

Small wonder, then, if confusion reigns. What if there had never been any "prophets"?

What if people had just allowed these "prophets" to spout away on their soapboxes on a Saturday night and then ignored them? Would there have been the terrible religious wars and events that have occurred over the years?

Do we need a set of commandments to tell us right from wrong? Why can we not have faith in ourselves to lead good lives? We have a choice to either practice good living at home and lead by example or get into a routine of going to a building with a crowd of other people and performing some religious ritual. The point being that we do need to have faith in something. Our lives can have purpose without commitment to some religion or church. There certainly are things that cannot be explained but that is because we haven't been around long enough to have that knowledge. The idea that there is some all-seeing, knows everything "being" looking down on us is tough to accept especially as we move forward into space exploration and the discovery of similar planets to ours. Yet, for most people, when they visit a church or chapel for whatever reason, they feel very emotional, whether it be the occasion or maybe a particular hymn being sung but there are genuine emotional feelings. Nicholas Wade, in his book 'The Faith Instinct' seems to think that religion is necessary for society and that religion may even be a brain function which has evolved as man has evolved. Being a member of a religious group encourages the member to behave, morally, ethically etc. or become an outcast. Religion imposes costs on its members in order to deter people who seek to enjoy a religious community's benefits without contributing anything to its costs. Free riders can be highly corrosive to a community's cohesion. By raising the cost of entry, a religious community excludes free riders and ensures that its members are committed. A high price of entry also raises the level of trust amongst its members.

There is, in a sense only one religion. Or, to put it more exactly, all religions are related to one another because all belong to the same family. But people are much attached to the particular features of their own faith and are more likely to dwell on its differences with other creeds than with its commonalities. This is somewhat similar to languages. Just as present-day languages all stem from the same tree, so too may religions. A totally novel religion has little chance of success but the easiest way for a new religion to start is as a sect of an existing one. People commit to religion during the formative years of puberty often during emotional initiation rites and most people are unwilling to abandon the religion they learned in childhood and adolescence. This is also likely to be the religion of their family and friends.

Nevertheless, religion has been, and is, the source of way too much confrontation between nations and families, and this confrontation which has evolved into war on numerous occasions, far outweighs any good that may have been achieved. This is because man has interfered and interpreted writings and scriptures and history books to suit his monetary and power needs, and done it all in the name of God.

One of the problems is that the Bible, especially the Old Testament, and the Quran' are full of violence-of-God traditions that are deemed "sacred" texts. An excellent book titled "Is Religion Killing Us" by Jack Nelson-Pallmeyer contends that these texts are the fundamental problem and they are not an issue of misinterpretation. In other words it is not a case of people taking passages out of context and twisting them in order to justify violence. He goes on to present ideas for alternative ways to approach "sacred" texts so that we can learn from both their distortions and their insights concerning God and faith. Doubt is also an issue that is discussed in his book and is pretty much a theme, a driving force, of this book. "Is Religion Killing Us?" is a provocative book but the author is a well respected university professor and his thoughts and arguments are well documented. What is still unclear is why there are so many "violence-of-God" "sacred" texts in the Bible and Quran to begin with. Surely if they had not been written in the first place then they would not be available for people to use them to justify their violent acts. Or is Mr. Nelson-Pallmeyer saying we should be selective in deciding whether to believe or to doubt certain passages? Is this not pretty much the gist of what has already been said, that man has interpreted these "sacred" writings to suit his own needs? So is the answer then, for everybody to just ignore the bad stuff and concentrate and apply the good stuff? Well isn't that hunkydory, may as well re-write the whole bloody lot and be done with it!

The following are some additional comments on the origins of Judaism:

Judaism has its roots in the agricultural past and the language, religion and culture of the ancient Israelites were derived from the Canaanites, the West Semitic peoples who inhabited the southern Levant, now Syria, Jordan and Israel. Hebrew is a dialect of Canaanite. Several festivals of the Israelite and Jewish liturgical calendar are adaptations of Canaanite agricultural festivals.

Virtually all main stream scholars acknowledge that true monotheism emerged only in the period of the exile in Babylon in the sixth century BC as the canon of the Hebrew Bible or Old Testament was taking shape. The problem with the Bible is the conflicting evidence or lack of archaeological evidence prior to 622 BC to corroborate the Bible narrative. Especially the episodes dealing with the deeds of the patriarchs, the exodus from Egypt, the conquering of the Promised Land of Canaan by Joshua, the glorious reign of King David and the magnificent palace of Solomon.

Some details even conflict with the evidence outright but the most substantive evidence contradicting the story of the Promised Land come from archaeology. Joshua's conquest of Canaan and sacking of its cities should have left telltale ruins dateable to around 1200 BC. Some 40 cities that the Bible says were conquered by Joshua have now been identified and excavated. Only three have archaeologists found possible evidence of pillage at the right date. Jericho at that time had no walls to fall to the blast of Joshua's trumpet. It seems quite likely there was simply no Israelite conquest of most of Canaan. But if there was no conquest of Canaan, there was no exodus from Egypt. Perhaps a small group of people escaped, and their story became extended to apply to everyone, but the Israelites as a people did not escape from captivity in Egypt. They did not spend 40 years traversing the Sinai desert nor did their army conquer Canaan. There is no need for a Moses, and the fact that his name is not mentioned in the earliest reference to the exodus, Miriam's song of the sea (Exodus 15), could suggest he is a later construct. The same may be true of Joshua, given that his feat of conquering the Promised Land seems to belong to legend, not history.

So if the Israelites never invaded Canaan, how did they come to occupy it? Because they **were** Canaanites and always had been. That is the conclusion at which archaeologists have finally arrived after many decades of bafflement. As contemporary scholars have wrestled with earlier theories, as well as with new archaeological data, most of them have come to agree on one point: at least a good part of what was to become the future nation of Israel had probably always been there.

The central theme of the Hebrew Bible is that Yahweh intervened in history in order to free the Israelites from captivity in Egypt, lead them across the desert and deliver the Promised Land into their hands. But this uplifting theme is not supported by the available historical and archaeological evidence.

During the Iron Age (1150-586 BC), the Israelites lived in two small kingdoms, those of Israel and Judah, set in the region's central hill country. The two kingdoms led a precarious existence because they lay in a buffer zone and battleground between the two regional superpowers of the time, ancient Egypt to the west and Assyria to the east.

In or around 722 BC, the kingdom of Israel was destroyed after Hoshea, the last king, defied the Assyrians. The Assyrian king Sargon 11 records how he resettled 27,000 Israelites in Assyria and repopulated Samaria, the capital of Israel, with people from elsewhere in his empire. Many other Israelites migrated to the southern kingdom, Judah, and the population of its capital, Jerusalem, then a modest highland town, increased fifteen fold.

A century later a major shift in the balance of power in the region led Assyria, between 640 and 630 BC, to withdraw from Palestine. Seeking to take advantage of the new situation, Jerusalem planned to regain the territory of the northern kingdom and unite it with Judah's. The Bible was its political and religious strategy for doing so.

On the political front, the Bible presented a stirring nationalist theme, that the Israelites had left Egypt in the exodus, conquered Canaan and established a glorious unified kingdom under kings Saul, David and Solomon. It would be legitimate for the current king of Judah, Josiah, to take over the remnants of Israel, ran the Bible's message, because he would be reestablishing the united kingdom of David.

On the theological side, the Bible argued for centralizing Yahweh-worship in Jerusalem, for national observance of Passover and other festivals, and for the suppression of local cults, which the Bible's authors saw as symbolic of chaotic social diversity.

The Bible's message of political and theological unification was reinforced with a thorough rewriting of history. The Israelites had been defeated by the Assyrians whenever their kings had affronted Yahweh by worshipping other gods, the Bible stated. They had enjoyed political success, and would do so again in the future, as long as they worshipped Yahweh correctly. The new, centralized kingdom of Judah and the Jerusalem-centered worship of Yahweh was read back into Israelite history as the way things should always have been.

History, unfortunately did not take the course the Bible's authors had hoped for. Warfare erupted and Josiah was killed by the Egyptians before he could unite the two kingdoms and a few years later the Assyrian empire itself was shattered by the Babylonians. The new Babylonian king, Nebuchadnezzar, set out to reconquer the territory the Assyrians had held. He captured Jerusalem in 597 BC. Following a rebellion he destroyed both the city and its temple in 587 BC and deported much of the population of Judah, with many prominent citizens to Babylon.

The Bible was rewritten to explain away these events and incorporate them into some acceptable form for the Israelite people to use as a religious and moral future reference .

Though the Bible failed in its political goal of uniting the two kingdoms, it succeeded beyond measure in creating a sacred text that bound believers together in a common purpose. The Israelites would surely have disappeared as a distinct people, along with the Midianites and Amonites and Moabites, had they not grown into a cohesive community through allegiance to their new sacred text.

The text elicited in the strongest possible way the innate propensity for religious behaviour. It satisfied the desire for contact with the supernatural by supplying an alternative in the form of prophets who had communed with the deity. It furnished a theological explanation for the historical disasters that continued to rain down on a small people caught between warring superpowers.

The binding force of the new religion was almost too strong. Jews resisted Roman rule and the requirement for adherence, or at least lip service, to the Roman state religion. They were drawn into a succession of disastrous revolts against Roman rule, which led to the destruction of Jerusalem and the second temple by the Roman general Titus in 70 AD. But Judaism also preserved Jews as a people during the diaspora around the Mediterranean world, a process already in train but accelerated by the loss of the temple. And remarkably, Judaism inspired two major sects, Christianity and Islam, as well as more recent offshoots such as Mormonism, all of which have claimed access to their own special revelations that update and improve on that of the Old Testament.

So much for the early history of Judaism and the Bible but what about religion and warfare? Did religion evolve as a response to warfare? People throughout history have died in defence of their religion putting their own and their family's interests second to what they considered a higher cause. But though religion has been deeply shaped by warfare, it is not inseparably linked to it. Religion provides a social cohesion, militant if necessary, that a society or its leaders may use to support an aggressive or pacific policy. This is clear from the beginning of Judaism when the divine directive, in the case of the Promised Land for the chosen people, was for a thorough ethnic cleansing.

Unlike Judaism, Christianity began as a religion of nonviolence as befitted a small sect subject to intermittent persecution by Roman authorities. But around 350 AD Athanasius, the Patriarch of Alexandria, decreed that though it was wrong to kill, it was lawful for a soldier to kill the enemy. As it began to share in the responsibilities of empire, the once peaceful church became habituated to the use of force in the state's interest.

The third monotheism, Islam, has generally proved somewhat less adaptable than Christianity. Far from beginning as a persecuted sect, Islam was shaped as a religion of empire, with Muslim Arabs as the rulers and conquered peoples subjected to various forms of discrimination. Jews and Christians were allowed to practice their religions but accorded a second-rank "protected" status which though it conferred certain rights, still left them subject to a poll tax and other burdens.

"Qu'ranic discussions on fighting made it clear that religious rewards, that is the joys of paradise, were more important than material success" writes the historian Hugh Kennedy. In these ways, the Koran provided the ideological justification for the wars of the Muslim conquests.

Looking back at the relationship between religion and warfare, each of the three monotheisms have followed a different course. Judaism started as an expansionary creed and transformed itself into a pacific one after defeat. Christianity began as nonviolent, became an aggressive religion of empire, and was then somewhat neutralized after the rise of secular states. Islam was created as a religion of empire but has generally not yet found an easy role in a secular state.

No consistent relationship emerges between religion and warfare, other than that religion is a potent instrument that can be wielded by rulers in many ways. Here then is the problem. Rulers have been quick to realise that religion may be quickly invoked causing it to be used to energize a society and motivate troops. It is usually no more a cause of war than are weapons, both are primarily means of war. Even when the formal cause of war is expressed in terms of religion, the underlying motives are usually secular.

Nevertheless religion can still be listed as a source of war and strife. Notably the wars between religiously defined groups in Palestine, the Balkans, Northern Ireland, Kashmir, Sudan, Ethiopia and Eritrea, Sri Lanka, Indonesia and the Caucasus. In these places religion has been the **explicit** cause of literally millions of deaths in the last ten years.

The vivid presence of religion in all these conflicts certainly raises the question of whether some of them might have been reduced or avoided did religion not exist. But the issue may not be as straightforward as it seems.

Before the modern state was secularized, religion, politics and warfare were much more intimately intertwined and it was scarcely possible to separate them in many circumstances.

Researchers at the University of Bradford in England assessed 73 major wars for the role played in them by religion and concluded that only in three did religion play an extremely intense role-the Arab conquests of 632-732, the Crusades of 1091-1291 and the Protestant-Catholic wars of the Reformation. In 60 percent of wars they found that religion played no part at all. The researchers say "There have been few genuinely religious wars in the last 100 years". Religion may play a less central role in many modern wars, and secular powers conduct many wars without any official citation of a religious pretext but religion, in addition to its offstage role in modern countries in preparing soldiers for battle, is frequently evoked as a rallying cry. In contexts like this, religion seems more of a means of war than an end, and its contribution to casualty is much like that of weapons. Weapons may provoke a war if one country's build-up of arms is deemed an intolerable threat by its adversary. But in general weapons are seldom considered a prime cause of war, and much the same is true of religion. Some wars have been classed as just, many wars regarded as defensive, at least by the country that is attacked. Many are unavoidable, especially for neighbours of an expansionist power. Religion's contribution to just and defensive wars may be regarded as positive.

It may therefore be a wasted effort to draw up a scorecard for religion and its positive or negative contributions to warfare because as stated previously religious behaviour evolved to induce social cohesion and thereby govern two essential human social behaviours, self-restraint within a society and aggression, if necessary, towards members of other societies. The groups whose members developed the strongest and emotional ties among one another were best able to prevail. These ties, forged in religious training and ritual, embedded in human nature its contradictory qualities of self-restraint and aggressiveness.

People today are the descendants not of those who lost out in these unremitting struggles but of the victors. We have inherited the capacities for extreme hostility, cruelty, even genocide, toward those who threaten us, along with the capacities for loyalty, love and trust toward members of our own community. An individual may be one or the other, but societies and nations are inextricably both.

Two serious assaults on religious belief, or at least on the three text-based monotheisms, have been the rise of scientific knowledge, including especially the theory of evolution, and "higher criticism", the analysis of Bible texts spearheaded by nineteenth-century German scholars such as Julius Wellhausen.

Science has provided an increasingly comprehensive explanation for the material world, one which is now largely complete, in principle if not in detail, except for singular events such as the origin of the universe and the origin of life on Earth and even these two events are much closer to explanation. This knowledge has gradually eroded a major intellectual pillar of religious belief.

A second challenge to religious belief emerged from the nineteenth-century practitioners of higher criticism who showed that the Bible, far from being the inerrant product of divine inspiration, was cobbled together by a number of different human hands whose varied stitching, once pointed out, was all too visible. This was particularly painful for Protestant faiths. Catholicism and Judaism had always emphasized their official interpretations of the sacred text rather than the text itself. But a major element of the Reformation was Luther's belief in the literal truth of the Bible, a tenet firmly endorsed by the Puritans.

Catholics and Jews, after the initial shocks had worn off, adapted to the challenges from higher criticism by interpreting parts of their sacred texts metaphorically. They were followed by liberal Protestants. But the conservative wing of the Protestant movement, instead of hedging its commitment to the literal truth position in light of all this new information, remained unmoved.

Halliday, Fred, 100 myths about the Middle East, The religions of the Middle East- notably Islam, Christianity, Judaism - are, if their holy texts are consulted, 'religions of peace'.

"The whole argument about religious texts as being for or against a particular form of action, be it war, capitalism, environmental protection or the equality of men and women, is mistaken.

Religious texts, beyond certain core items relating to belief, contain variant prescriptions and judgments about social and political life including armed hostility between groups and states. For those who want to use them, there are passages that condone, when not encouraging, violent acts towards people who are not members of the group in question, and which can be and have, in modern times, been used to justify terrible atrocities. The choice is not given by the religion or text; the authority for 'peace' in the Middle East is not given by religion, nor by the men authorised to represent and interpret it, but is a result of explicit and contemporary decisions".

Alternatively, the religions of the Middle East are 'religions of war'.

"This is the obverse simplification to that found in the preceding myth. The same argument applies: there are plenty of bases in the holy texts, histories and traditions of Middle

Eastern religions on which to construct a modern politics and international law of cooperation, respect for the general rules of war and coexistence between states and communities.

Moreover, while it is possible - as is often the case - to use religious authority to legitimise modern nationalism and the claims of specific nationalisms (Zionist, Iranian, pan-Arab, local Arab), there is also in each religion a strong element of universalism and appeals for a shared humanity within a recognition of the positive diversity of peoples, cultures and religions".

These then, are my concerns, 'Why has there and continues to be, so much violence associated with religion? Is violence the reason why so many derivatives or sects have been formed? Is it possible that those contriving to form a new slant on religion were trying to achieve a peaceful approach to faith and worship of our one God?' This is a highly commendable act but kind of falls apart when it becomes a case of "you will obey or else!"

Is it possible that over the last five thousand years we have compounded a religious issue that never really existed except in the warped minds of a few? Did we allow myths to cloud our senses? Were we so desperately looking for and in need of some spiritual signs to lead us in the right direction? Did we really need God to tell us right from wrong?

The book really needs a timeline which reflects my concerns but trying to construct an appropriate one is a task all by itself. So much of the early history of the people who are associated with that land is reliant on the Bible and so much of that Bible history has and is being continually contradicted by archaeological evidence. Biblical dates and ages have been conveniently manipulated to better fit in with the scribes' desire to produce a logical and acceptable commentary.

Hopefully the choice of Chapters will suffice as a simplified timeline but there is a section at the end of the book called 'Timeline Discussion."

1
IN THE BEGINNING
5000 BC to 3200 BC

In the beginning, long before the Bible was written or even conceived, history began. This beginning is in the sense of written history, where man became "civilized", if that word can ever be applied to man. "Civilized" being the fact that man started recording his life.

This event happened in Uruk in the land of Sumer in Mesopotamia which is now called Iraq and is generally dated to around 3100 BC as evidenced by the excavation of hundreds of small clay tablets inscribed with crude pictographic signs.

In fact we are going to go back further to around 5000 BC and beyond, into prehistory as it is called, just so the complete picture is apparent.

We are not going to dwell too long on these early years, suffice to say that the land was gradually being populated as man began to migrate to areas that afforded the best living conditions. The Fertile Crescent, as most of this area would eventually be known, was a narrow strip running from the Nile valley northwards through Palestine, passing through the west and north of Syria then turning south-eastwards trough Iraq, would become hugely popular and in great demand. The fertility of the earth being a condition left after the preceding Ice Age.

Throughout prehistory, the Holy Land figures as a terrestrial bridge, joining Asia with Africa and the great Arabian Desert with the

Mediterranean Sea. The frequent contact with neighbouring lands, and the significance and function of the area in ethnic migrations and shifts of nomadic groups, appear to be the main reasons for the particularly varied and creative spirit that is perceptible in the vestiges left us by Prehistoric Man.

Over the course of this period different cultures evolved, to a degree the cultures were determined by the condition of the land itself. Archaeological finds show that there was an Age of Hunting and Gathering and a transition to the Age of Early Agriculture with sub cultures arising within the main groups.

Over the years these cultures evolved, even outpacing similar cultures in Europe and some major sites have been uncovered in the vicinity of Jericho and Jerusalem and because of the finds there was obviously communication between the sites. Trade existed even in these very early years in the Holy Land but food producing activities acquired more importance in the local economy and farming villages began to spring up and so the population of the Middle East grew markedly, social units became larger and were more densely concentrated. In fact settlement at Jericho is thought to extend as far back as 9000 BC. Evidence from in and around Jericho suggest further diversification of cultures as a consequence of successive waves of new peoples entering the Holy Land from the surrounding areas, the coastal zones of Syria to the north and southern Anatolia, the central Jordan valley to the south, even as far south as Egypt and possibly Mesopotamia to the east.

Of course, religion, or at least modern religion as we know it, had not reared its ugly head yet so man was left to gradually become 'civilized'.

2
CIVILIZATION WITH THE WRITTEN WORD
3200 BC to 2200 BC

It is the mythology of the Sumerians rather than their theology which is worth noting here. The Sumerians recorded the oldest myths known to us – stories about the creation that would be echoed many centuries later in the Creation myths in Genesis. But the most astonishing parallel between the Sumerian myths and the Biblical myths is the story of the Flood.

Several versions of the Sumerian Flood story have been found over the years, all of them pre-dating the Bible. The most sophisticated version forms part of an epic poem about one of the ancient semi-legendary kings of Uruk, a man called Gilgamish. In one episode, he pays a visit to the only human survivor of the Great Flood, the Sumerian Noah, in effect, on whom the gods bestow immortality. The story he is told is so close in its detail that the Biblical Flood story was obviously borrowed directly from the much earlier Sumerian original. The individual names may be different but the specific parallels are unmistakable.

The Bible outlines with precision the genealogy of the patriarchs. It reports that Terah, the father of Abraham, was a ninth- generation descendant of Shem, the oldest of Noah's three sons. There is no historical record other than the Bible itself that tells of Abraham but many details of the patriarchal account in the Book of Genesis are supported by the political, cultural and religious history of the second-millennium BC Near East.

Before we follow Abraham's Trek in Chapter 3 let's see where the land of Canaan is. The ancient land of Canaan covered present day Israel, The West Bank and Gaza Strip (as well as adjoining coastal lands and parts of Lebanon and Syria). Owing to the absence of written records we have no sure way of establishing the ethnic origin of the inhabitants other than that noted in Chapter 1, but archaeological evidence indicates close ties with Egypt and as will be stated later, Canaan was a huge empire by 2200 BC primarily because of its location and the fact that two international caravan routes bisected the country .The fact that Canaan was already an established and prosperous empire would make it attractive to immigrants wanting to improve their way of life and lends credence to the theory that Abraham's was a fairly peaceable integration.

3
ABRAHAM'S TREK AND THE BELIEF IN ONE GOD
2200 BC to 1700 BC

The Bible will be used extensively as a historical reference book even though events in the Bible occurred hundreds and even thousands of years before they were written about, and the story is going to start with Abraham as he is generally considered the head patriarch and his name does not appear in any other book, history or otherwise, other than the Bible.

Some background to Abraham's lineage according to the Bible, because this has some bearing on his journey to Canaan, is that Abraham was of Shem's line. Shem was a son of Noah as was Ham. The root of the word Semite is Shem. A son of Ham was Canaan and Canaanites were the descendants of Canaan. Abraham's descendants are considered Semitic, Canaanites are considered non-Semitic.

Worth noting here is the fact that excavations have been taking place at a site in Syria called Tell Mardikh some 40 kilometres south of Aleppo (Aleppo being about 375kilometres north of Damascus), where thousands of inscribed clay documents have been found. They reveal the existence of a mighty Canaanite empire in Syria that also embraced Palestine around 2400 BC. Its capital was at Tell Mardikh, an ancient, all-but-forgotten city called Ebla.

What makes it doubly sensational for "Biblical archaeology" is that the greatest of the kings of this mighty empire of Ebla had the same name as one of the legendary ancestors of Abraham, his great-great-great-great-grandfather: a king called Ebrum, or Ebrium, which is the same as that of the Biblical Eber (Genesis 11), the eponymous ancestor of the Hebrews.

Also found in the tablets were a number of personal names and place names with which the Bible would later make all familiar: places like Sinai, Gaza and Jerusalem and people like Abraham, Ishmael, David, Saul and most astonishingly of all Israel.

Abraham's father, Terah or Terach was from "Ur of the Chaldees" according to the Bible. Ur is located approximately fifty kilometres south of Uruk. "Ur of the Chaldees" is a misnomer; Ur was one of the original city states of Sumer from around 3500 BC and did not become associated with the Chaldaens until a thousand years or more after Abraham was thought to have been born there. Abraham was thought to have been born around 1996 BC and contrary to popular belief he may have been quite an educated city dweller as excavations from that area have shown that Ur was quite a prosperous city, being on one of the main trading routes of that time and Terah was apparently a dealer in idols. No evidence of only one God at this time obviously.

Abraham's father, Terah, decided to move the family north to Haran which is now in modern-day Turkey. Why he would consider moving if he was doing ok where he was, is a mystery. Maybe there was considerable unrest in the area at that time and Ur's power was waning. He may have wanted to move his family to a safer haven. The fact is, that in this same area today are villages that still have names of Abraham's grandfather and great-grandfather, Nahor and Serug.

According to the Bible Abraham had already been chatting to God and maybe or maybe not, had persuaded his father to get rid of all his idols. There is no clear date as to when they set out from Ur but his father, Terah, seemed to figure that they should and would go to Haran where they stayed for some time. Terah died in Haran and according to *Genesis*, Abraham lived there until he was seventy-five years old which would be around 1921 BC. At some point Abraham was told by God to get moving again and that Abraham would be told somewhere down the road where he was going.

How many of them were there by this time? Difficult to estimate because the numbers and ages of people in the Bible are ridiculously silly and have obviously been manipulated to make the stories seem plausible.

From Haran, Abraham is said to have travelled south to Shechem, in Canaan, some 1000 kilometers with his family or clan. This journey now seems more suited to Abraham being a nomadic herdsman than an original well-to-do city dweller. Was there a journey at all? Was Abraham a historical figure at all?

At some point during this part of the journey, Abraham's wife, Sarah, had grown old without bearing a son, so Abraham took a second wife, Hagar. She gave birth to Ishmael, whereupon Sarah also conceived a son, Isaac. Sarah demanded that Abraham banish Hagar and Ishmael from the tribe, and according to the Koran, they went south to Mecca. Abraham and Isaac continued their journey in Canaan.

The debate really centers on the question of when the Bible account was written, and why. There is a general and uncritical presumption that the Patriarchal stories were handed down orally, more or less unchanged, around the camp fires of the nomadic Israelites until they came to be written down at the time of David and Solomon in the tenth century BC. This is contested by scholars who believe that the first books of the Bible were written considerably later, during the period of the Babylonian Exile in the sixth century BC. They reach their conclusion on grounds of textual and literary criticism chiefly but also on social grounds: the trauma of the Exile created the need to construct and articulate a comprehensible historical past, a perspective of history which would give a meaningful context to the identity of the Hebrews and their special relationship, as they felt, with their god.

If Abraham made it to Canaan, The Promised Land, he must have been a ripe old age by then and we assume his clan were relatively few in number so he would have no difficulty in merging with the existing society. Remember Canaan at this time was a huge empire and Abraham probably already had a few distant relatives living there. A grandson of Noah, was Canaan (father was Ham), and the Canaanites were supposedly descendants of Canaan. But the earliest inhabitants of Canaan came from all over the Arabian Peninsula, so they were inevitably a mixed bunch. It appears that Abraham was surprised that there were already people living in Canaan because God had said He would lead him to the Promised Land. Why Abraham was surprised to find people already there is strange because Canaan was a huge empire and had been for a long time. Everybody knew that!

It was obviously a peaceful integration, Abraham may even have been able to worship his one god without any interference from the authorities. The powers that be seemed more lenient then in permitting people to worship whatever took their fancy.

Did Abraham's tribe integrate into the existing society or did they settle in the hilly region of Canaan? This was long before the Assyrians came to power but were there other forces to consider?

Everything appears relatively calm, peaceful and civilized at this point in time. (1870 BC?) Just a family or tribe emigrating to another part of the country to better themselves, then famine struck.

Genesis describes the patriarchs as leaders of a large and wealthy nomadic clan which favoured non-involvement with the more densely settled urban populations. Nevertheless they rested in the vicinity of the few mountain towns that there were (Shechem and Hebron) or in the Negev (Beersheba and Gerar), receiving protection of their rulers though taking care not to assimilate with them but to preserve their nomadic way of life.

According to *Genesis,* famine occurred fairly soon after their arrival in Canaan so off they went on their travels again. When did famine strike – 1870? And the famine was obviously so bad that they had to pack up and go to Egypt.

It appears that there were still not too many in Abraham's tribe, his wife, Sarah, and Lot, his brother's son. Off they went to Egypt, and because of some shenanigans and deceit concerning his wife and pharaoh they were thrown out of Egypt but were much richer by far than when they arrived. But still there were not too many of them, according to the Bible but apparently they had herds of cattle and sheep and Abraham and Lot's herdsmen quarrelled over who should have the best grazing so they separated. Lot made his choice to settle near the city of Sodom and four other cities and Abraham moved from Bethel to Mamre.

What date are we at now? Did Abraham only spend three months in Egypt? Is it still 1870 BC?

As of now there has been no discovery of a city resembling Sodom.

There was a constant struggle between the "kings" of the various tribes at this time. The stronger ones trying to enslave the smaller. Nothing has changed obviously. Sodom was looted and Lot and his family were carried off by one of these kings into captivity so Abraham rounded up a bunch of warriors and took up the chase. Long story short, he walloped them, saved Lot and his family and was rewarded by the King of Sodom who had flown the coup to save his sorry ass.

But what did Lot do? He went back to live near Sodom. Needless to say Abraham turned down all the spoils of plunder he was offered.

It seems that Abraham's god at this time was not too concerned who got whacked even if it was Abraham who was doing the whacking. Kind of makes one wonder why the Ten Commandments didn't make an entrance at this time. Might have saved a few lives.

There is more confusion here as it may be that at this point in time, Abraham took a second wife, Hagar who gave birth to Ishmael and eventually Sarah gave birth to Isaac. Not as noted at an earlier time.

Obviously warfare and strife was an accepted and natural state of affairs during this period of time and Abraham's one god was privy to all the dastardly goings on but must have just been content to let things take their course.

Returning to the famine - one of the ten God appointed famines for the chastisement of men. The first of them came in the time of Adam, when God cursed the ground for his sake; the second was this one in the time of Abraham; the third compelled Isaac to take up his abode among the Philistines; the ravages of the fourth drove the sons of Jacob into Egypt to buy grain for food; the fifth came in the time of the Judges, when Elimelech and his family had to seek refuge in the land of Moab; the sixth occurred during the reign of David, and it lasted three years; the seventh happened in the day of Elijah, who had sworn that neither rain nor dew should fall upon the earth; the eighth was the one in the time of Elisha, when an ass's head was sold for fourscore pieces of silver; the ninth is the famine that comes upon men piecemeal, from time to time; and the tenth will scourge men before the advent of Messiah, and this last will be "not a famine of bread, nor a thirst for water, but of hearing the words of the Lord."

The famine in the time of Abraham prevailed only in Canaan, and it had been inflicted upon the land in order to test his faith. He stood this second temptation as he had the first. He murmured not, and he showed no sign of impatience toward God, who had bidden him shortly before to abandon his native land for a land of starvation.

As noted previously, this is the time, in Egypt, when the shenanigans happened with Abraham's wife Sarah and Pharaoh and resulted in Abraham and his family returning to Canaan much wealthier than before, mostly paid off by Pharaoh to get rid of the plague that had been cast down on him for his intended indiscretions. He bestowed rich gifts upon the husband and the wife, and they departed for Canaan after a three months' sojourn in Egypt. The date is now 1870BC and with Abraham on his return from Egypt is his wife Sarah, sons Isaac and Ishmael and possibly Isaac's wife Rebekah (b.1938 BC). Also Lot (Abraham's brother's son) and his family.

Is it automatically assumed that all of Abraham's extended family now worship only the one God? This is still a period where the norm is the worship of multi- gods and idols. Is there now a dormant period until the next famine which is termed the Great Famine and lasts seven years and results in Isaac going to Gerar, the land of the Philistines under King Abimelech. The Bible says this was a generation after Abraham. Would this be about 1741 BC? If Abrahams's death was 1821 BC? This would suggest the period of the Great Famine was 1741-1734 BC.

During the period 1870 BC to 1741 BC Abraham and his family lived in Canaan, probably near Beersheba as the Bible refers to the burial of four couples in the Cave of the Patriarchs also called the Cave of Mahpelha situated in Hebron, north of Beersheba and south of Jerusalem. The four couples are Adam and Eve, Abraham and Sarah, Rebekah and Isaac, Jacob and Leah. Abraham and his wife Sarah have two sons, Ishmael (b.1910 BC) and Isaac (b1896 BC). Isaac marries Rebekah and they have twin sons, Jacob and Esau (b.1836 BC), Esau being the first born.

Jacob's life seems to be one predominated by his having to flee from one circumstance after another. After he stole Esau's birth right, Esau was so angry with him that he planned to kill him, and so his mother, Rebekah, sent Jacob away to her brother, Laban, in a foreign country. After living with Laban for several years and marrying two of his daughters, Leah and Rachel, Jacob began to be rich because he figured out a way to make his sheep and goats produce more and stronger offspring than the livestock of his uncle Laban. The Bible tells us that Jacob became rich as Laban became increasingly poor. And then, one day, without telling Laban his plans, Jacob packs up all his belongings, his wives, his children, his servants, his livestock, and takes off, fleeing from Laban. After a couple days, when Laban found out that Jacob had fled, Laban pursued him. He was upset because so much of his wealth left with Jacob, but also because Rachel had stolen an idol and taken it with her. When Laban caught up with Jacob, he accused him of stealing, and Jacob, not knowing that Rachel had stolen the idol, denied it. When Laban was unable to find the idol, he and Jacob made a peace agreement, and Jacob traveled on with his belongings, returning to the land where he grew up.

Here, according to the Bible, is evidence of idol worship still, so obviously there are mixed feelings amongst Abraham's family and descendants regarding monotheism.

One more time, though, we find Jacob and his clan moving on--this time because his daughter Dinah, whose mother was Leah, had been talked into having sex with a gentile man in the area, and two of her brothers then planned to take revenge on the clan. Jacob bought a plot of land from the people of Shechem and lived there for some time. One day his daughter Dinah went to attend a festival of the women of Shechem. Shechem son of Hamor, the king of the city of Shechem, saw her and fell in love with her. He kidnapped her and forced her to stay and live with him. Jacob and his sons were horrified and humiliated by this outrage, and they were determined to avenge their sister's dishonor. They knew that even according to the laws of Shechem, this outrage was a crime punishable with death, and that the entire population of Shechem had had a share in the crime. Simeon and Levi fell upon Shechem and slew all the men, including Hamor and his son Shechem.

Jacob rebuked his sons for this action. Soon a large army of Canaanites gathered to fight Jacob and his sons. But Jacob and his father Isaac prayed to God, and the Canaanite kings became frightened and resolved to return to their cities without a fight.

Jacob moved to Hebron where his father Isaac lived. There he resided many years. Then he returned to Shechem because the land was best suited for his large flocks. Again the kings of Canaan united to destroy the children of Israel. But with the help of God, and under the heroic leadership of Judah, the small army, composed of Jacob's sons and servants, defeated the seven kings who had united against them. The rest of the Canaanite kings were now so afraid of Jacob's sons, that they preferred to make peace with them. Jacob returned to Hebron, but his sons stayed with the herds near Shechem.

Isaac died at the age of one hundred and eighty in 1716 BC, and his sons Jacob and Esau laid him to rest in the Cave of Machpelah. Esau took all the wealth and movable possessions of his father and settled in Seir, while Jacob inherited the land of Canaan, as God had promised.

This is now after the period of the Great Famine (1741BC -1734 BC), maybe something amiss with the chronology (not surprising), but Jacob's family is now complete, with the twelve sons (tribes) of Israel beginning to take shape. Jacob loved his second youngest son, Joseph (b.1745, d.1635 BC), who had also inherited the exquisite beauty of his mother Rachel and spent much of his time teaching him everything he had learned from his father and grandfather. Thus the relationship between Joseph and his brothers became strained.

This is the beginning of the story of Joseph and his time in Egypt, according to the Bible narrative. Joseph's brothers found the opportunity to capture him and eventually sell him to a passing caravan of Ishmaelite merchants. The Ishmaelite merchants sold Joseph to a caravan of Midianites, who brought him to Egypt.

Joseph's is a popular story and the Bible makes much of the interpretations and meanings of the various episodes during his life. Joseph, having impressed Pharaoh with his ability to read dreams and forecast events becomes a high ranking official in Egypt and when famine occurs again, Joseph has already built up a stock of supplies to enable Egypt to survive this hardship. The famine was so extensive that Canaan was also affected and Jacob sent ten of his sons to Egypt to buy grain and at the conclusion of events, eventual reunion of the brothers and much rejoicing took place. Jacob brought his entire clan to settle in the land of Goshen on the Nile delta which Joseph had obtained for them, this migration to Egypt occurring around 1706 BC. Jacob breathed his last at the Biblical age of 147 in 1689 BC and Joseph and his brothers continued to prosper in Egypt with Joseph eventually dying in 1635 BC. Joseph told his children Ephraim and Manasseh, both of whom who had been blessed by Jacob previously, "God will visit you and bring you up out of this land to the land which he swore to Abraham". Centuries would pass before this would happen, but Joseph, at least is demonstrating his faith in the "one God".

At this stage, in Egypt in 1630 BC, pretty much altogether are the "12 Tribes of Israel" – Gad, Ashe, Rueben, Simeon, Levi, Judah, Issachar, Zebulan, Joseph, Benjamin, Dan and Naphtali.

These were the sons of Jacob (Israel) by his two wives and two concubines. His favourite wife, Rachel, gave him his favourite son Joseph, the last of the patriarchal figures and the one by whom events are set in motion that bring the Israelites not to permanent settlement in the Promised Land as might have been suspected but to seemingly permanent slavery in Egypt.

This period in history, Abraham sojourning in Egypt, God making himself apparent to Abraham, the years passing with bondage in Egypt and the development of the twelve tribes is strictly Bible as there is no archaeological evidence or even mention in Egyptian history to support any of the stories. But something of great importance obviously did happen to Abraham and his descendants which would forever maintain the identity of the Hebrew people or tribe(s) where other tribes of that period have long since vanished from history.

One of the most prominent Hebrew religious leaders, Moses is regarded as the most important prophet in Judaism, Christianity, Islam, the Bahá'í Faith, Rastafari and Chrislam, amongst many other faiths. He acted according to the request of God and freed the Jews from the brutality and slavery they were experiencing under the Pharaoh of Egypt. He was also God's chosen one to receive the Ten Commandments, which were given to him in the form of a stone tablet. The Ten Commandments still hold importance in the world.

Moses was born in 1576 BC (this is not the date given in Exodus). During this time, Hebrew were slaves in Egypt and as per the order of Egyptian Pharaoh, all newborn Hebrew males had to be drowned in the river Nile, so that no one could grow up and fight against him. Jochebed, the mother of Moses was reluctant to adhere to the wishes of Pharaoh. She hid him in a basket by the side of the River Nile. After about three months, when Jochebed could no longer hide the child, she put him in an ark and cast him on the waters of the Nile, thus abandoning young Moses to God's protection. According to Biblical account, Moses' sister Miriam observed the basket until it reached the place where Pharaoh's daughter Thermuthis was bathing. Spotting the baby, Thermuthis asked her maidens to fetch it for her. She took Moses with her and kept him, as though he were her son. After a few unsuccessful attempts to nurse the baby, Miriam proposed if Thermuthis would like a Hebrew woman to nurse the baby. This is when Jochebed was asked to nurse Thermuthis adopted baby, her own son. Eventually, he became Thermuthis' son and a younger brother to Rameses II, the future Pharaoh of Egypt.

Though Moses grew as an Egyptian prince, he never forgot that he was a Hebrew. One day, while on his trip to the countryside, on seeing an Egyptian killing a Hebrew, he could not control his temper and killed the Egyptian. He buried the dead body in the sand. However, everyone came to know about it. Moses came to know that the Pharaoh was likely to put him to death for killing an Egyptian. To save his skin, impressed by Moses' brave act, Hobab adopted him as his son and got his daughter, Zipporah, married to Moses. Moses was made the superintendent of his herds as well. For four decades, Moses stayed in Midian and lived as a shepherd. He was also blessed with a son, Gershom. One day, while Moses was leading his flock to Mount Horeb, he came across a burning bush. Coming closer to it, he realized a voice coming from it. It is believed that God spoke to him from the bush, revealing His name to Moses.

Moses fled to Midian. There, he saved seven of Hobab's daughters from a band of rude shepherds. God instructed Moses to return to Egypt and free the Hebrews from slavery. He also taught him to transform a rod into a serpent and also to inflict and heal leprosy. He also gifted Moses with the blessing that he could change river water to blood, by pouring on dry land. As per Quran, Moses was instructed to accomplish two goals - invite the Pharaoh to accept God's divine message and give salvation to the Hebrews. Moses left, along with his brother, Aaron, for Egypt. It is believed that the Pharaoh of the Oppression had been replaced by a new Pharaoh, known as the Pharaoh of the Exodus, as the former had died.

This new Pharaoh would have nothing to do with Moses and Aaron and their requests for observance of Hebrew traditions and the wishes of their one God; therefore over a period of ten days Egypt was subjected to ten plagues. The tenth plague was the most dangerous of all and caused death of the first-born male of all Egyptian families. Getting immensely upset on losing his son, the Pharaoh asked the Hebrews to leave Egypt.

So the Hebrews departed but then Pharaoh changed his mind and sent his army after them. This then is the story of Moses, leading up to the Exodus, which occurred in 1496BC.

Even though there is doubt that strict monotheism in Abraham's people existed during this time, by God's appearance to Jacob and then Moses in various episodes, there is a developing of the one God faith and this development would continue all through the Egyptian period into the time of the Exodus.

Again, whether the Exodus did or did not occur is irrelevant because the Hebrew people have survived against all odds.

As shown above, the Bible describes all this in a tremendous amount of detail. The Biblical scribes obviously wishing to make this part of Hebrew history one of the foundation stones on which their faith would be built. The fact that nothing like this narrative probably happened did not seem to dismay them but this is the history that they wanted to convey to future generations. Anything less startling would get lost somewhere.

Continuing on then with the escape from Egypt, the Hebrews needed to shake off the Egyptian army pursuers and this they did apparently by parting the waters of the Red Sea, crossing safely then allowing the waters to return to normal just as the Egyptians were in the middle of the crossing. Again, maybe an exaggeration but it would be interesting to know how this rag-tag assembly of slaves escaped the clutches of one of the best armies of the time.

The "Exodus" or escape from Egypt, more than any other story in the Bible, served to solidify the faith in God that was developing but it was to be a very long journey before the Jewish people would be able to call themselves "The Children of God".

4
THE ORIGINS OF THE HEBREW TRIBE AND THE JEWISH RELIGION
1700 BC to 1300 BC

The tribes' faith is now to be tested in the Sinai Desert that most desolate place that lies between Egypt and Canaan and their journey, since destroying the Egyptian army, seems to have been one continuous moan and groan and God has tried to placate them by performing miracles through Moses but was fighting a losing battle. It's all so easy to believe in something or someone when all is going well but when things are not going well somebody has to take the blame. So obviously Moses and the "new" God were the scapegoats and when Moses was called by God to spend some time on Mount Sinai the tribes resorted to their 'idol' ways.

Moses was on the Mountain receiving The Ten Commandments from God. These sacred words were chiseled on stone and most scholars have come to the conclusion that the original sentences were are all bluntly brief in the manner of "You are not to murder" – so brief in fact that each one may have been but one word that is, utterly primitive, basic injunctions on the order of "No-Kill," "No Steal," "No Lie." In fact The Bible does not use the word 'Commandments', it portrays them as 'Words' but there is no disputing or questioning the meaning of the Commandments or Words. Although God destroyed the stones because of the sins of the Israelites, who had wasted no time in breaking as many Commandments as possible, especially while Moses had been on the Mountain, a copy had been made (another miracle). Here is the modern text of the Ten Commandments:

- You shall have no other gods before me.
- You shall not make for yourself a carved image- any likeness of anything that is in heaven above, or that is in the earth beneath, or that is in the water under the earth.
- You shall not misuse the name of the Lord your God in vain.
- Remember the Sabbath day, to keep it holy.
- Honor your father and your mother.
- You shall not murder.
- You shall not commit adultery.
- You shall not steal.
- You shall not bear false witness against your neighbor.
- You shall not covet your neighbor's house; you shall not covet your neighbor's wife, nor his male servant, nor his female servant, nor his ox, nor his donkey, nor anything that is your neighbor's.

Moses had led "God's people" for many years. Because the Israelites did not obey God while they were in the wilderness, God did not lead them straight into the land He had promised them. The trip from Egypt to their new home should have taken the Israelites only DAYS, but instead, they wandered in the desert for 40 YEARS. All of that time, God PROVIDED everything the Israelites needed. After forty years of wandering, the entire generation of Israelites who were delivered from slavery had died, except Joshua and Caleb. It was the children who had been born during the wilderness years who were left now.

Joshua had been Moses' helper since Joshua was a young boy. Moses was not allowed to enter the Promised Land because on one occasion he had disobeyed God in front of all the Israelites. Moses asked God to appoint another man to lead the Israelites .God told Moses to lay his hands on Joshua, and Joshua received the spirit of wisdom .God told Joshua that he would be the one to lead the Israelites into the Promised Land .God warned that after the Israelites were in the Promised Land

and their lives were going very well, they would turn from God and begin to worship other gods. God said He would burn with anger and many disasters would come upon the people. So for a time Moses was the spiritual leader and Joshua was the warrior leader.

The statement has already been made and accepted - The Bible and archaeologists do not tell the same story. The conquest of Canaan is a good example: The Bible says Joshua conquered the whole region leaving no survivors (Josh 10:42 cf. 11:16-23). Archaeologists say Israel "emerged" from among the Canaanite peoples without a conquest. They say this because there is evidence of neither culture change nor comprehensive conquest. Archaeology has apparently proved the Bible wrong. Major differences between the Bible and archaeology are: There is no evidence of the destruction of Egypt by plagues at the Exodus. There is no evidence of a forty-year wilderness wandering, no evidence of a rapid and complete conquest by Joshua, and no evidence for a wealthy internationally trading kingdom of Israel under King Solomon, etc.

Properly interpreted archaeology should tell the same story as the Bible. The big details should match: plagues destroyed Egypt, Israel wandered forty years in the wilderness, Israel attacked and conquered Canaan, etc. Most recent archaeologists deny there is substantial evidence for these events. The explanation for some of the differences of opinion could arise from the Biblical chronology which, as has already been noted, is most misleading. The Biblical scribes tending to manufacture dates of events to describe and fit into history as would benefit future Jewish generations. Egypt holds a unique place in archaeology because its chronology is "fixed" and early. Egyptian chronology is fixed because it is based on written records tied to fixed risings of the star Sirius dating to *c.* 1870 B.C. Biblical scholars say Biblical archaeological chronology is tied to Egyptian chronology. Sir Flinders Petrie discovered pottery-dated stratigraphy, the ability to date debris layers by pottery. Pottery was similar over large areas and changed slowly with time. Pieces of broken pottery had little value and therefore generally stay in the strata where they first fell. Petrie linked the ubiquitous pottery pieces to Egyptian chronology. Linking the relative pottery chronology to the fixed Egyptian chronology, Biblical chronology became fixed. This is the debated issue.

Following on from The Ten Commandments and Mount Sinai, God used Moses to lead the Israelites out of slavery in Egypt. God had promised to lead His people through the wilderness into a wonderful land. God said the land was good and spacious, and it would be flowing with milk and honey (Exodus 3:8). The Israelites were now east of the Jordan River. God was going to give the Israelites the land that was west of the Jordan. The land was not a land without people, though. The land was already home to the Canaanites, Hittites, Amorites, Perizzites, Hivites and Jesusites. These people had homes, cities, and armies. Do you think all of these people would just give up their home land when the Israelites came? The Israelites will have to participate in many battles to conquer this land. God told the Israelites that they would conquer all of these people, and they must destroy them totally (Deuteronomy 7:1).

There is a whole book in the Bible devoted to Joshua. Many readers of Joshua are deeply troubled by the role that warfare plays in this account of God's dealings with his people. . It tells how God commissioned his people to serve as his army under the leadership of his servant Joshua, to take Canaan in his name out of the hands of the idolatrous and dissolute Canaanites (whose measure of sin was now full; see Ge 15:16 . It further tells how he aided them in the enterprise and gave them conditional tenancy in his land in fulfillment of the ancient pledge he had made to Israel's ancestors, Abraham, Isaac and Jacob. Joshua is the story of the kingdom of God breaking into the world of nations at a time when national and political entities were viewed as the creation of the gods and living proofs of their power. Thus the Lord's triumph over the Canaanites testified to the world that the God of Israel is the one true and living God, whose claim on the world is absolute. It was also a warning to the nations that the irresistible advance of the kingdom of God would ultimately disinherit all those who opposed it, giving place in the earth only to those who acknowledge and serve the Lord. At once an act of redemption and judgment, it gave notice of the out outcome of history and anticipated the final destiny of humankind and the creation.

The battles for Canaan were therefore the Lord's war, undertaken at a particular time in the program of redemption. God gave his people under Joshua no commission or license to conquer the world with the sword but a particular, limited mission. The conquered land itself would not become Israel's national possession by right of conquest, but it belonged to the Lord. So the land had to be cleansed of all remnants of paganism. Its people and their wealth were not for Israel to seize as the booty of war from which to enrich themselves (as Achan tried to do,) but were placed under God's ban (were to be devoted to God to dispense with as he pleased). On that land Israel was to establish a commonwealth faithful to the righteous rule of God and thus be a witness (and a blessing) to the nations. If Israel became unfaithful and conformed to Canaanite culture and practice, it would in turn lose its place in the Lord's land -- as Israel almost did in the days of the judges, and as it eventually did in the exile.

Where Deuteronomy ends, the book of Joshua begins: The tribes of Israel are still camped on the east side of the Jordan River. The narrative opens with God's command to move forward and pass through the river on dry land. Then it relates the series of victories in central, southern and northern Canaan that gave the Israelites control of all the hill country and the Negev. It continues with a description of the tribal allotments and ends with Joshua's final addresses to the people. The theme of the book, therefore, is the establishment of God's people Israel in the Lord's land, the land he had promised to give them as their place of "rest" in the earth (1:13,15; 21:44; 22:4; 23:1; see also Dt 3:20 and note; 12:9-10; 25:19; 1Ki 5:4 . So the Great King's promise to the patriarchs and Moses to give the land of Canaan to the chosen people of his kingdom is now historically fulfilled (1:1-6; 21:43-45).

The above few paragraphs are common knowledge but in today's political and religious turmoil how can those wars and conquests be seen as anything but what they really are – "Ethnic cleansing" – and the present day Western world going 'tut –tut' isn't that awful.

Joshua's warmongering exploits rank right up there with the likes of Alexander the Great, Ghengis Khan and Hannibal. The justification being that it is God's land and the land is paganized and needs to be purged so that the Children of Israel can fulfill their destiny.

So much for the Ten Commandments.

The most detailed account of the conquest is in the Book of Joshua, which presents it as a single campaign on the part of an organized nation following a definite plan laid down by its leader, Joshua, son of Nun, successor to Moses as commander of the Children of Israel. It is clear that Joshua, who was of the tribe of Ephraim, was involved in the wars of 'The Sons of Rachel' (or 'House of Joseph') and led them in battle. Joshua's time can be attributed to the first wave of tribes. The second wave, 'The Sons of Leah', among them the tribes of Judah and Simeon crossed the middle Jordan and continued on to Judah and the Negev, as recounted in the first chapter of Judges. Judah captured Jerusalem but was powerless to hold it and it fell to the Jebusites, a people of unknown origin, which occupied the city down to the time of David.

This is the period which is regarded as the time in which the Hebrews first came together as a nation. A handful of tribes of common origin, and sharing the same faith and tradition, united to build their future in the country which they had chosen to be their homeland.

The problem with storytelling especially when retelling orally from generation to generation, even though the events actually happened is the tendency to exaggerate or even wander altogether away from the original. Maybe this is why the Bible goes to so much trouble to list genealogies in a way that leaves no doubt as to the authors intention to write an accurate chronicle of events.

The legendary "conquest" described with such bloodthirsty relish in Joshua as an overwhelming victory was probably not so much a conquest but more of an integration of peoples into an established area. Yes, there may have been some skirmishes but most of the tribes found homes in already ruined towns and villages or made new homes in the hill country of Canaan.

The conquest had its origins in the convulsions of the Egyptian-Hittite wars in the time of Ramses 11. The thinly populated border areas in the Holy Land were vulnerable to attack by desert rovers of many kinds. It seems that that the pharaohs could neither maintain order in these areas nor control the tribes and clans which fled from Egypt. According to Exodus 1:11, Pharaoh built and embellished the city that bore his name by pressing the Children of Israel into forced labour as was with the case of other clans and tribes at during this period..

At about this time, there were Israelite tribes dwelling at the oasis of Kadesh-Barnea, at the southern and of the Negev, and hovering on the borders of the Holy Land. Their attempts to move from the Negev due north were thwarted by the chain of fortified Canaanite cities in that part of the country. The problems they encountered at Hormah forced the Israelites to look for some other route inland.

After settling the central highlands and intermingling with the natives, the Israelites appeared to return to their misbehaving ways by worshipping some of the existing Canaanite gods and images. This period after Joshua's invasion is called the period of the Judges – local military leaders who also settled disputes between Israelites. Also during this period there appears a time of continuing settlement and consolidation in which Israelite warrior-farmers gradually spread out through Canaan in loose tribal confederations until in less than two centuries they occupied most of the Promised Land.

It appears that Joshua tried to keep his people on the straight and narrow path of worshipping their one God but as soon as he died they fell apart. Obviously there is a need for another spiritual leader.

Historical Setting:

At the time of the Israelite migration into Canaan the superpowers of the ancient Near East were relatively weak. The Hittites had faded from the scene. Neither Babylon nor Egypt could maintain a standing military presence in Canaan, and the Assyrians would not send in their armies until centuries later.

As the tribes circled east of the Dead Sea, the Edomites refused them passage, so Israel bypassed them to the east. However, when Sihon and Og, two regional Amorite kings of Transjordan, tried to stop the Israelites, they were easily defeated and their lands occupied. Moab was forced to let Israel pass through her territory and camp in her plains. Also the Midianites were dealt a severe blow.

Biblical archaeologists call this period the Late Bronze Age (1550-1200 BC).

Today thousands of artifacts give testimony to the richness of the Canaanite material culture, which was in many ways superior to that of the Israelites. When the ruins of the ancient kingdom of Ugarit were discovered at modern Ras Shamra on the northern coast of Syria, a wealth of new information came to light concerning the domestic, commercial and religious life of the Canaanites. From a language close to Hebrew came stories of ancient kings and gods that revealed their immoral behavior and cruelty. In addition, pagan temples, altars, tombs and ritual vessels have been uncovered, throwing more light on the culture and customs of the peoples surrounding Israel.

Excavations at the ancient sites of Megiddo, Beth Shan and Gezer show how powerfully fortified these cities were and why they were not captured and occupied by Israel in Joshua's day. Many other fortified towns were taken, however, so that Israel became firmly established in the land as the dominant power. Apart from Jericho and Ai, Joshua is reported to have burned only Hazor (11:13), so attempts to date these events by destruction levels in the mounds of Canaan's ancient cities are questionable undertakings. It must also be remembered that other groups were involved in campaigns in the region about this time, among whom were Egyptian rulers and the Sea Peoples (including the Philistines). There had also been much intercity warfare among the Canaanites, and afterward the period of the judges was marked by general turbulence.

Much of the data from archaeology appears to support a date for Joshua's invasion c. 1250 BC. This fits well with an exodus that would then have taken place 40 years earlier under the famous Ramesses II, who ruled from the Nile delta at a city with the same name (Ex 1:11). It also places Joseph in Egypt in a favorable situation. Four hundred years before Ramesses II the pharaohs were the Semitic Hyksos, who also ruled from the delta near the land of Goshen.

On the other hand, a good case can be made for the traditional viewpoint that the invasion occurred c. 1496 BC. The oppression would have taken place under Amunhotep II after the death of his father Thutmose III, who is known to have used slave labor in his building projects. The earlier date also fits better with the two numbers found in Jdg 11:26 and 1Ki 6:1, since it allows for an additional 150 years between Moses and the monarchy.

When it comes to the beginning of the actual conquest, there are two biblical versions, each recording a tribal migration. According to Numbers 33, the Israelites passed through Transjordan and the Plains of Moab to Jericho without any opposition. This would appear to have been an earlier wave of tribes at about the end of the fourteenth century or the opening of the thirteenth century BC. and this first wave fits the group of tribes known as the 'Sons of Rachel' or 'House of Joseph' – the tribes of Ephraim Manasseh and Benjamin. The second wave had to make a tour around Edam and Moab until they reached the Amorite border later in the thirteenth century BC. The second wave consisted of 'The Sons of Leah' – among them the tribes of Reuben and Gad, which settled in Transjordan

In the course of time, after the tribes acquired their respective portion of land there emerged a delineation of the boundaries and extent of Israelite settlement. The parts that the Israelites could not subdue, 'the land that remaineth', encompassed most of the fertile valleys and still left a number of enclaves in Israelite territory. The Canaanite cities, armed with the war chariots which the Israelites lacked, could arrest Israelite expansion along with the fear of Egypt whose influence was now confined to the Canaanite cities. Denied space to spread out, the tribes had to adjust their way of life to the cramped conditions. The territorial division of the country in this period had four principal centres of Israelite settlement, cut off from one another by areas inhabited by hostile populations. These were: Galilee, the central mountain region, the Judaean Hills and the Negev, and Transjordan. Archaeological excavations tend, by and large, to confirm the stages of the conquest and the approximate chronology as ascertained from contemporary sources but there are certain discrepancies, for instance the Biblical time of the destruction of the cities of Jericho and Ai (et-Tell, east of Beth-el) is questioned by the archaeologists.

The division of the country amongst the tribes was not the end of the process of settlement and many Biblical sources, especially the genealogical lists of clans and tribes affirm outright or hint at subsequent wanderings and migrations for different reasons.

5

THE ISRAELITES IN THE LAND OF ISRAEL
1300 BC to 1000 BC

Israel in Early Times - According to Hebrew tradition, 12 tribes entered Canaan from Egypt and conquered it, led by Joshua. Historical evidence from the Amarna tablets suggests that there were already 'apiru' (probably Hebrews) in Canaan in the time of Egyptian rule, some possibly with names such as "yakubu-el" (Jacob). The biblical account allots different parts of the land to the twelve tribes as shown in the map. Soon after, a kingdom was established, first under Saul and then under David. The maps are necessarily conjectures based on biblical narrative and supporting archeology.

2nd millennium BC - Egyptian hegemony and Canaanite autonomy were constantly challenged by such ethnically diverse invaders as the Amorites, Hittites, and Hurrians. These invaders, however, were defeated by the Egyptians and absorbed by the Canaanites, who at that time may have numbered about 200000.

In Egyptian records especially the ones concerning the Egyptian occupation of Canaan there is evidence of the presence of Israelite tribes. There are contradictions between biblical tradition and archaeological finds but let's try to make some sense out of it all.

The earliest known manuscripts of the Old Testament date from the Babylonian captivity in 586 BC. These were destroyed by the Syrians during the Jewish uprising in 168 BC.

Prior to 1947 the oldest known manuscript of the Old Testament was *Codex Cairensis* (AD 895) and the oldest complete text was *Aleppo Codex* (tenth century AD.) All that changed with the discovery of the Dead Sea Scrolls.

The importance of the Dead Sea Scrolls (dated from the first century BC to the first century AD) continues to grow and to be one of the most intriguing stories of modern times. Their value in the study of scripture is unparalleled.

Archaeologists have found scrolls of every book except Esther and have been able to fill in historical details about the life and times of the Essene community who were responsible for hiding the scrolls.

The significance of the biblical scrolls found at Qumran was not in the new information they provided, but in the general confirmation of the accuracy of the Masoretic text. The Qumran scrolls predate the previously known manuscripts, *Cairensis* and *Aleppo* =, by over a thousand years. In fact the text of the Dead Sea Scrolls confirmed much of the text used in our modern Hebrew Bible.

Obviously not all original manuscripts were destroyed by the Syrians in 168 BC. if the Masoretic text has been confirmed as accurate.

The ten tribes of Israel are (from North to South):

DAN, NAPTHAL, ASHER, ZEBULUN, ISSACHAR, JOSEPH, (subdivided into the tribes of MANASSEH and EPHRAIM), GAD and REUBEN (in Transjordan) and BENJAMIN (just north of the border with Judah – all of whom made up the Kingdom of Israel). The tribes remaining are Judah and Simeon who make up the Southern Kingdom of Judah.

The above is important because when the Assyrians descended on the Kingdom of Israel they carried off everything and everybody and they became "The Ten Lost Tribes". The Judeans of the Southern Kingdom would soon be known as the Jews.

As a people ISRAEL simply vanished.

Same thing happens to the Southern Kingdom of Judah because of their resorting back to the worship of false gods and idols. This time it is Nebuchadnezzar, king of Babylon, which has now eclipsed Assyria in the power politics of Mesopotamia, who levels the city (Jerusalem), and the temple and reduces the whole country to ruin and desolation.

The Ark is lost forever.

This all because the tribes strayed from God. The belief is that God had been telling them all through time he did not want material offerings, he just wanted their hearts, their spirit and the warnings had been there along with the threat of dire consequences.

Who is to say that the tribes would have been annihilated regardless of whom they worshipped? This was a time of warring nations and although the tribes may have been somewhat battle hardened they would be no match for the Assyrians or the Babylonians who had possibly decided that they needed to beef up their treasury and slave labour. It was that kind of time.

Let's go back a little, to the time when the tribes were settling in to their new homeland. Some cities, because of their fortifications, had not been taken over, leaving pockets of non-Hebrew areas all over the place. At about the same time as the Israelites were infiltrating into Canaan, the Sea Peoples, especially the Philistines were making their presence felt and they were going to make lives difficult for the Hebrews. Despite the popular belief the Philistines were a crude and depraved lot of heathens, (this belief encouraged by the Israelites because the Philistines dared to lay sacrilegious hands on the Ark of the Covenant,) they were not without their ideas of civilization. It is recorded that around 1190BC, Ramesses 111, Pharaoh of Egypt met and checked, both land and sea, a massive invasion by the Sea Peoples. The reason for the invasion was primarily famine, in fact as the famine continued, the whole Middle East was in turmoil. But after the defeat of the Sea Peoples, the Philistines were not annihilated but were put to work by the Egyptians, for example, manning the Egyptian garrison fortresses that commanded strategic trade routes, especially the Via Maris up the coastal plain of Palestine. The battles on land and sea had exhausted Egypt and whole Egyptian kingdoms rapidly disintegrated after the death of Ramesses 111 (c1170BC) and the Philistines became masters of the areas they had settled under Egyptian sufferance.

Around 1050BC is the expansion of Philistine power and prosperity and the Biblical story of Samson. Apparently the Hebrews (call them Hebrews for now because Israelites is confusing at this stage), had fallen into their ungodly ways again and were in the hands of the Philistines. It seems as though the Hebrews were having a tough time with their monotheism. It certainly would be interesting to be a fly on the wall in some of their houses at that time just to see how individual families were dealing with the one God issue, bearing in mind that the whole area, in fact the whole land were still praying and giving sacrifices to a multitude of gods and idols. It is important to remember that the Hebrews were farming the land and raising livestock and their calendar revolved around agriculture and the effects of the seasons. A lot of the gods and idols of the time, and had been for thousands of years, were related to the land and the people believed that if these gods were appeased then the harvests would be plentiful. Old habits die hard, and the fact that the Hebrews did not have a leader or king it is understandable that they would revert back to their old ways for the most part. Was that the case – who knows?

Back to Samson, he was born in the foothills of the mountains of Judah near Beth-Shemesh which is a kind of border country between the Philistines on the plains and the Hebrews in the hill country. After the treachery by Delilah, Samson was brought to Gaza. In ancient times Gaza was the southernmost of the Philistine cities, a site of great strategic importance as the last city in Philistia before entering the Negev desert. But again, no archaeological evidence has been found to confirm the story of Samson and his destruction of the temple.

The Philistines were growing stronger, they had a flourishing economy based on maritime commerce and had control over the overland coastal route, the Via Maris. They had a great army and a technology monopoly. A crisis came around 1050BC as the Hebrews attempted to stop further encroachment into their hill country by the Philistines and a battle was fought at Eben-Nezer. Eventually the Hebrews were annihilated and the Ark of the Covenant was captured by the Philistines. The Hebrew tribal league was in utter disarray, with their hill country occupied and their sanctuary destroyed but then along comes a man called Saul and a boy named David.

The story of King Saul and his tragic relationship with his former favourite, David, is an intensely passionate interplay of powerful and flawed characters. In Biblical terms, Saul represented the first ruler whom the Children of Israel were prepared to accept as a 'king' after the sporadic and unstable charismatic leadership of the Judges. It was his ultimately tragic reign that paved the way for the rise of the United Monarchy under David, and the creation of Jerusalem as the City of David.

The story of Saul's kingship starts around 1025BC when the fortunes of the Children of Israel were at their lowest ebb. The hated Philistines had captured the Ark of the Covenant, they had destroyed their ancient cultic centre at Shiloh and occupied their land. But at a place called Gilgal the tide began to turn for the Israelites because of Saul. Saul was leading his people, winning battles but was not without opposition, this was in the form of a prophet called Samuel who had reluctantly anointed Saul by popular demand of the people for a king. Samuel felt that they already had a king, namely God and they were taking a step backwards. Here we seem to have the first conflict between the idea of a secular monarchy and that of a divinely inspired tribal leadership through elders and prophets.

Forward now to the time when Saul meets David, this is all Biblical conjecture as even the Bible cannot agree on the version of events that leads to David's position of influence in Saul's court. What is apparent at this time is that the Hebrews are a warring nation and physically fighting for the land that they believe is rightfully theirs. Is this any different than the Philistines believing the same? Anyway the point being that the Ten Commandments have conveniently been put under the bed until such time as the Children of Israel have decided that they have achieved their goal.

David's is quite a story, from a leader in Saul's army he defects to the Philistines at one point but is spared the final treachery of taking the field against his own people and during this final battle the Israelites were completely destroyed, three of Saul's sons were killed and Saul, severely wounded, took his own life. This is really a sad tale, could there have been another way? Or is God saying this bloodthirsty path has to be followed in order for the eventual truth and light to be seen? There is archaeological evidence of military activity in that area dating to that period in history but obviously no corroboration of the Biblical accounts of Saul or David but as has been mentioned previously the Bible scribes believed they were transcribing the oral versions of actual events. What has become evident from scholars studying the Philistines is the standard of culture which they brought with them to Canaan – a highly sophisticated culture which was superior to that of the Israelites and the Canaanites and which is expressed in their pottery, their buildings and their social organization. It is hardly surprising that the Israelites found them such a formidable foe and wrote bitterly about them afterwards.

David emerged from his exile amongst the Philistines and was acclaimed and anointed King of the southern state of Judah at the ancient shrine of Hebron but Saul's military commander, Abner, threw his support behind one of Saul's sons, Eshbaal, who formed a kind of government across the Jordan River, laying claim to the northern kingdom of Israel. For the first time, the concept of 'Judah 'and 'Israel' as separate integral entities now begins to emerge. David's star was now in the ascendant. Both Abner and Eshbaal were conveniently murdered and so the dynastic claim of the House of Saul to the throne came to an abrupt end and the elders of the northern state of Israel now came to David and offered him the kingship of Israel as well. This change of events worried the Philistines who were still a force in the land despite all that was happening and they mobilized an expedition against David, but he had learned a lot during his time with the Philistines and he beat them at their own game, two decisive victories in fact which caused the Philistines to simply cease to be a major power in the land. They would be limited to their original territories in the coastal plain of Philistia and David was free to develop his own political power-base from which to build up an empire, which he did, eventually making his capital the Jebusite city of Jerusalem.

David's Royal City seems to have been rather small even by the standards of the day but with great ceremony he brought the Ark of the Covenant that had lain for many years discredited after its ignominious capture and return by the Philistines, to Jerusalem and installed it in a tented shrine he had prepared. Are the Ten Commandments about to be resurrected? No, apparently not, as David's exploits would attest, but apart from his discreditable personal conduct (obviously excused) his political strokes were masterful eventually extending his empire all the way from the borders of Egypt to the Euphrates.

David's last years as king were clouded by a series of palace intrigues and profound personal sorrow when his favourite son, Absalom, rebelled against him and was killed. The mystery still remains as to how all of David's sons were disqualified from inheriting the kingdom except for Solomon, his son by Bathsheba. The picture of David given in the Bible is that of a man who had fulfilled his primary purpose in establishing a united Hebrew monarchy for the first time, but whose sins were so great that he was not considered worthy to carry out the ultimate function that Jerusalem was to have in the eyes of later commentators, namely to be the religious and political capital of the Jews through the building of a Temple. But David prepared the ground and made all things possible for his illustrious successor, Solomon. He purchased a piece of land just outside the city, on a high place, where his son Solomon would consummate the Biblical narrative by building the First Temple.

Solomon does build the temple but all is not well in the land. Although the southern kingdom of Judah had accepted the principle of a centralized monarchy, it seems that the northern kingdom of Israel had never become reconciled to the House of David or to the loss of their tribal independency. In particular they bitterly resented the penal taxation and forced labour that Solomon imposed on them in order to carry out his grandiose schemes. When Solomon eventually died around 920BC after forty years on the throne, this pent up resentment boiled over, the United Monarchy fell apart and the Empire disintegrated. The leader of this separatist group was King Jeroboam and he led Israel out of the Union with Judah within weeks of Solomon's death.

What was the religious state of things at this time? Was the worship of the 'one' God, the new monotheism the mainstream? The Bible devotes an awful lot of space to this time – Samuel 1 and 2 and the Book of Psalms for instance. Did David lead his people in the worship of God? Was he the author of all the poems and psalms the Bible has credited him. Hard to imagine a bunch of scribes sitting down hundreds of years later and writing all that stuff so there must be some sort of truth at least in the origins. Yet no mention anywhere except in the Bible. The one thing that does place David above the rest is the fact that he brought the Ark of the Covenant to Jerusalem but was this a political move? A masterstroke in fact which consolidated David's place in Israel's history. But what of the rest of the Hebrew population? Are they still practicing animal sacrifices and praying to any number of gods and idols who they thought may just be listening? If only there were some other historical indication of this momentous religious change that is supposed to be happening. Let's move on.

6
ISRAEL DIVIDED AND THE JEWS EXILED
1000 BC to 500 BC

So far there is nothing about the Hebrews or Israelites, or whatever name is appropriate for them at this stage, to suggest their behavior is any different from any of the other numerous peoples in that part of the world except as the Bible would have us believe otherwise. The Ten Commandments have been completely ignored. The Bible scribes have simply inserted God into their writings because that is how they wanted future readers to imagine and actually believe was the history of The Children of Israel up to that point.

Or is something being missed here? There is no evidence, even in the Bible, of a peaceable approach to resolve concerns, after all, the Twelve Tribes WERE the invaders and the instigators of death and destruction to an established land, yet all we read about are military conquests. No diplomatic concessions, no forgiveness, no charity. Nothing to suggest that the God we all want to believe in, is hard at work convincing everybody that the chosen path is the correct one.

But the question nags – Why did Abraham, in the beginning, uproot his established family, in an established and prosperous city and make an incredibly arduous journey into the unknown if not for God' voice? Was it God's wish that they physically fight to take control of the Promised

Land? God, like everyone else, knew the Promised Land was occupied and prospering quite splendidly. Surely God's intent was not to make an example of these people for their improper worshipping ways, they didn't know any better. This all flies in the face of everything taught to us as children, or maybe that doctrine didn't come along until Jesus made his appearance. Small wonder that Jesus was welcomed with open arms as the 'Saviour'.

Solomon's successor, his son Rehoboam, decided he would try to seek confirmation as king of Israel as well as Judah. But the northerners, the Israelites proper, said no way, after the taxes and slave labour that Solomon had imposed on them not too long ago. In fact they demanded that the penal taxation of Solomon's later years be removed, but Rehoboam threatened them with even heavier impositions. The Israelites promptly repudiated the Union and declared themselves a separate state. They lynched the chief tax collector and sent Rehoboam scurrying back to the safety of Jerusalem. No brotherly love here. In his place they appointed, as the first king of a separatist Israel that mighty man of valour, Jeroboam. Alas, this was the start of two hundred troubled years for the kingdom of Israel, which would end with its annihilation around 720 BC, by the Assyrians.

Prior to the Assyrian campaign though, Jeroboam had fortified the city of Shechem and made this the new capital of Israel. Shechem was always a highly strategic center throughout the history of Palestine, being located where important trade routes from Egypt and Jerusalem converged. It was also always a significant cult center in Hebrew tradition as it was Shechem that Abraham was said to have stopped when he first arrived in Canaan and where Joshua was said to have assembled the victorious tribes after his conquest of Canaan. Part of the fortifications built by Jeroboam, a formidable gateway facing towards Judah, can still be seen but the real enemy at this time was not Judah but Egypt. Around 918 BC, maybe a bit earlier, the Egyptian army swept through Palestine under a resurgent new Pharaoh, Sheshonk 1 (Biblical Shishak). The Bible seems to indicate that it was only the northern kingdom of Israel that was targeted but Egyptian records make it clear that both Judah and Israel were devastated. Isn't it strange that Egyptian records have been found to confirm this onslaught but nothing else regarding the Bible stories?

According to the Bible, Jeroboam had spent a deal of time in Egypt during Solomon's reign, having been at odds with Solomon over one thing and other then returned to become King of Israel by popular demand of the people and maybe it was because of the Egyptian connection that he decided to establish a religious cult to rival that of Jerusalem. Maybe he had a premonition of an attack by the Egyptian army and thought that this may help to keep him safe, so he gave official royal status to two ancient cult sanctuaries at opposite ends of the realm, the one at Bethel near the southern border and the other at Dan at the extreme northern edge of the country hard up against the present frontier with Lebanon. It appears that the Jerusalem religious cult at this time was establishing itself as a monotheist society? Confined to the city or spreading all over? This new religion by Jeroboam established at Dan and Bethel was a throwback to the early days of the Exodus with calves of gold and the burning of incense and blood sacrifices. What was the extent of this return to old religious ways? Actually few scholars believe that Jeroboam introduced idol worship but he undoubtedly touched a deeply responsive chord in his people. 'Deviant' cult practices seem to have been much more widespread than the Bible would have us believe.

Moving on to King Omri of Israel (circa 930 BC), and his son Ahab and Ahab's wife Jezebel; again it seems that the Bible scribes were prejudiced against Ahab and Jezebel probably because Jezebel introduced the worship of her Phoenician god Baal but it was under Omri and Ahab that the kingdom of Israel reached its peak of strength and political importance. Omri also has the distinction of being the first king of either Israel or Judah to be mentioned by name in the contemporary records of other states. It was Omri who built a new capital of Israel called Samaria and Samaria gradually lent its name to the whole region and its inhabitants would become known as Samaritans. Ahab has his own place as a builder of some importance which the Bible reluctantly gives him some credit and some of his structures may be on a par with Solomon's achievements. One of his rebuilding projects was the city of Megiddo, which is the future site of Armageddon.

The 'prophet' Elijah makes his appearance in the reign of Ahab and Jezebel, he was the implacable enemy of Jezebel and her Phoenician religion. This was the Elijah who "ascended to heaven in a whirlwind and a fiery chariot" on his death but his hatred of Jezebel was perpetuated through his disciple and successor Elisha. Two of Ahab's son reigned for a short while after Ahab's death but the real power behind the throne seems to have been Jezebel. About 865BC the religious opposition to her exploded in a military coup, Jehu the charioteer was appointed king in the name of the Lord by Elisha (not sure how he managed that) and Jezebel along with her son King Jehoram of Israel and his cousin King Ahaziah of Judah were brutally murdered. But that was just the tip of the iceberg, the whole of the royal family and court of Israel was exterminated then the chief priests and worshippers of Baal were butchered and the temple razed to the ground. Jehu's usurpation inaugurated a period of perilous weakness for Israel that lasted for fifty years and the southern kingdom of Judah was also undergoing a period of weak and unstable government during this period. However, in the eighth century both kingdoms enjoyed a remarkable resurgence of power and prosperity under two rulers – King Jeroboam 11 in Israel (786 BC-746 BC) and King Uzziah in Judah (783 BC-742 BC). The two states were at peace with one another and trade flowed until about the middle of the eighth century BC when the Assyrian super-power emerged. The Assyrians were the most violent and ruthless conquerors the Middle East had ever seen and they erased the Kingdom of Israel from the map of history for ever and the cities of Judah would be no more.

The Assyrians had been threatening for some time prior to their main invasion and some smaller states had formed a coalition of some sort to either prepare a better defense against the threat or to even decide to pay homage to the potential invaders but nevertheless the Assyrians came and destroyed. The Kingdom of Israel was overrun and organized into three Assyrian provinces and very large numbers of the inhabitants were deported to other parts of the Assyrian empire while the southern kingdom of Judah was allowed to remain intact because Judah had placed herself under Assyrian protection at the price of a huge tribute. The ten lost tribes of Israel disappeared from history and this is such an important historical event because, did Israel forfeit their claim to this land by being annihilated? The land was repopulated with foreign deportees from Syria, Babylon and Arabia who no doubt, over time would consider this their home. Once again Judah escapes the fate of deportation by becoming a vassal state but by doing so is able to rebuild and launch a major religious reform during King Hezekiah's reign and to sweep away the creeping paganism that had been tolerated prior to his reign. Should this episode be given more credit for preserving the monotheistic claim than is normally given? But Hezekiah's rise in popularity and religious reforms came to the attention of the Assyrians who had been preoccupied with battles elsewhere and Sennacherib attacked Judah with full force and was particularly brutal in his treatment of prisoners, the fortunate ones being led off to slavery and exile. The ones that could escape made their way to Jerusalem for safety and excavations have shown that the population of Jerusalem almost trebled overnight by the refugees from the first Assyrian attack on the northern kingdom of Israel and then from the second onslaught of the Assyrians on the southern kingdom of Judah. Sennacherib never did lay siege to Jerusalem, he returned to Nineveh even though he had demanded unconditional surrender from Hezekiah who had apparently tried to bribe Sennacherib with a huge tribute of gold and silver which had literally drained the treasury and stripped the temple of its remaining gold and silver. But the Assyrian grip on Palestine did not slacken and after Sennacherib's death, his son Esarhaddon was determined to extend the Assyrian empire even further, which he did and Lower Egypt fell to the Assyrians. At this point in history the power of the neo-Assyrian empire was at its zenith, the state of Israel had been obliterated and the state of Judah was completely under Assyrian rule. This means that Assyrian gods dominated the temple in Jerusalem and yet within fifty years the Assyrian empire would collapse and vanish, Judah would find a brief respite or independence but a new super power was rising – Babylon.

As Assyrian control weakened during the time of Josiah, King of Judah (Josiah being the great-grandson of Hezekiah), there are indications that he was a notable religious reformer and excavations have shown, for example, in Arad, in southern Judah that Josiah was attempting to adapt some of the features of the Jerusalem temple and there appears to be evidence of his orders to close down provincial shrines and cultic centers.

But storm clouds were gathering on the horizon and Josiah would not be allowed to continue his monotheistic reforms unfortunately. In 626 BC Babylonia revolted and resumed its independence and in 614 BC the Babylonians, together with the Medes from Iran advanced north up the Tigris against Nineveh which was utterly destroyed and within three years all opposition had been wiped out and Assyria was finished forever. Tragedy struck Judah in the year of 609 BC too when King Josiah tried to stop and Egyptian army marching north through Palestine to aid the last beleaguered Assyrians, he was killed in battle, his army was defeated and it was the end of Judah's independence.

In 604 BC King Nebuchadnezzar of Babylon came to the throne and after clearing out the last of the Egyptian forces from Syria he set out to make Babylon the most magnificent city in the world. In fact he was so busy with his building projects that he had failed to realize that Judah was becoming an irritant probably because at that time, about 597 BC, Judah had a young king, Jehoiachin, who was maybe being taken advantage of. Anyway in that year Nebuchadnezzar made a token assault on Judah and carried off the young king along with ten thousand captives including the best tradesmen in Judah. This was the first deportation from Judah, and ten years later, because of the continued rebelliousness of Judah under the puppet king, Zedekiah, the Babylonian army marched again. Jerusalem was blockaded and the other fortified cities of Judah fell one by one. Jerusalem held out for eighteen months but eventually fell in 586 BC or 587 BC and Nebuchadnezzar showed no mercy. The city was burned to the ground, the temple with its sacred Ark of the Covenant was looted and utterly destroyed and thus the First Temple, Solomon's Temple, came to an end. Now the second great deportation took place of approximately 20,000 leaving Judah a shambles and the captives became internees of the Babylonians.

This is by far the most important event in all of Israel's history as it is known that certain Hebrew writings were produced in exile and literary and historical traditions were reshaped, in fact there is no evidence that their captivity was entirely disagreeable. Little is known about the Jews in exile (the Jews being remnants of the Judeans of the Southern Kingdom, but in the course of their sojourn in various corners of the ancient world, some Jewish refugees, relying on the trading skills they had developed during the monarchy made new fortunes and became reluctant to leave their new homes. The period of exile therefore marks the beginning of the Jewish diaspora, a period that has never come to an end.

The exile did come to an end through Cyrus the Persian.

Is it correct in assuming that some remnants of the Ten Lost Tribes of the original northern Kingdom of Israel may have survived their captivity and integrated with the Judeans of the Southern Kingdom in Babylonia especially after it appears that captivity was not a really great hardship? Even though the Jews (Judeans of the Southern Kingdom) had already been renamed the Children of Israel is it possible that the years in captivity were spent gathering the tribes together one more time so that when the time came that they were allowed to depart and 'go home' there was representation of the original twelve tribes? Or did historical animosity among the tribes prevent any gathering of the 'clans"? The Book of Ezra in the Bible lists names and numbers which seem to indicate that there was quite a gathering once word got around that they were free to go and reading between the lines it appears that during the captivity they had been allowed to congregate and practice their 'one God' religion. (see note 1) Cyrus was of the opinion that he had been appointed by God to build a new temple in Jerusalem so who better than the captives who had been forcibly taken from there? The Book of Ezra states that the whole assembly numbered 42,360 and not all went back to Jerusalem but some returned to their original cities.

Note 1.

There are two schools of thought on the 10 tribes in Jewish circles:

(1) They're lost and will some day be reunited with Judah (The minority point-of-view):

"The people known as Jews are the descendants of the Tribes of Judah and Benjamin, with a certain number of the Tribe of Levi. So far as is known, there is not any further admixture of other tribes. The Ten

Tribes have been absorbed among the nations of the world. The Jews look forward to the gathering of all the tribes at some future date" (Dr. Hertz -- Chief Rabbi of the British Empire. 1918).

"While not a link is missing of the historical chain so far as the romance of the House of Judah is concerned, the Israelites who were subjected by the Assyrian power disappear from the page of history as suddenly and completely as though the land of their captivity had swallowed them up...the Ten Tribes are certainly in existence, all that has to be done is to discover which people represent them" (**The Jewish Chronicles**, May 22, 1879).

"The captives of Israel exiled beyond the Euphrates did not return as a whole to Palestine along with their brethren the captives of Judah; at least there is no mention made of this event in the documents at our disposal...In fact, the return of the ten tribes was one of the great promises of the Prophets, and the advent of the Messiah is therefore necessarily identified with the epoch of their redemption" (**Jewish Quarterly Review**, Vol. I -- 1888, pages 15, 17).

"Until the arrival of the Prophet Elijah and the Messiah, no member of any of the Ten Tribes shall be accepted (for the purpose of marriage) into the Jewish people" (Rabbi Rafael Eisenberg, **A Matter of Return**, p. 138).

> **(2) They intermarried and were absorbed into surrounding nations and races. They'll never return (The majority point-of-view):**

"The people were transported eastward, and a new population was brought in westward. The transported Israelites became the "ten lost tribes"; in reality these were absorbed by the people of the lands to which they were transported and they disappeared" (**The Hebrew Scriptures** by Samuel Sandmel, p. 20).

"Thus were the people led away into distant provinces of the [Assyrian] empire and became colonized with strangers, and the Kingdom of Israel became a tale that is told" (**ISRAEL: A History of the Jewish People** by Rufus Learsi, p. 79).

"…but in general it can be said that they disappeared from the stage of history" (**Encyclopedia Judaica**, vol. 15, p. 1004).

"These are the Ten Lost Tribes; lost not as a jewel is lost on the road, perhaps to be found again, but as a drop of wine is lost in an ocean of water, dissolved, gone" (**Eternal Faith, Eternal People**, by Leo Trepp, p. 14).

"The Ten Tribes of Israel were not even permitted like the sister kingdom of Judah, to bequeath to later ages…the memory of rich and varied destinies. They were irretrievably lost" (C. and A. D. Rothschild, **History and Literature of the Israelites**, Vol. 1, page 489).

"The Jews do not claim to represent the Twelve Tribes for the Ten Tribes never returned from captivity and are lost to history" (Rabbi Aaron Werner, when asked by Dr. Schiffner, '**Do the Jews represent all 12 tribes**').

"So, to condense this massive summary all down to one sentence: the ten lost tribes were conquered, and, like almost every other conquered people in the ancient world, lost their separate identity and were assimilated away into the sands of history" (Collective summaries from Eli Barnavi's **Historical Atlas of the Jewish People**, Judah Gribetz's **The Timetables of Jewish History**, Joseph Telushkin's **Biblical Literacy**, and the **Encyclopedia Judaica**).

7
RETURN FROM EXILE AND PERSIAN RULE
500 BC to 400 BC

When the Babylonians are defeated by the Persians, the Persian king Cyrus issued an edict in 538 BC, almost exactly 70 years after the prophecy of Jeremiah, allowing the Jews to depart. A small group return to their ancestral home and more will follow in the years to come. This is a different generation than the one that left and they brought with them books, old and new. The Torah reached its final form soon after, entwining the oral literatures of Judah and Israel.

There is without a doubt some beautiful literature in the Old Testament. Whether it actually belongs to the person the Bible attributes it to is debatable but it is difficult to believe that a bunch of scribes sat down at a later date and composed it all from scratch.

The Jews gave the world a whole new vocabulary, a whole new landscape of ideas and feelings that had never been known before. Over many centuries of trauma and suffering they came to believe in one God and because of their unique belief in monotheism, the Jews were able to completely overwhelm the warring and contradictory phenomena of polytheism. They gave us the conscience of the West, the belief that this God, who is one, is the still small voice of conscience, the God of compassion and the God who will be there for all of us, no matter what.

The Bible writers fail to provide a clear or coherent account of the time or times leading up to their release from captivity by the Persian King Cyrus. One incident only is made known and that is "Belshazzar's Feast" (Daniel 5), where a mysterious hand appears and writes on the wall and Daniel the Jewish magician was the only one who could translate the words. Belshazzar at the time was the king of Babylon and his Empire was at such an all-time low that Cyrus and his army walked right into the city of Babylon unopposed and Cyrus was actually welcomed as a liberator. Cyrus was so liberal in his religious views that he restored all the gods to their former sanctuaries but he adopted the chief god of Babylon, Marduk, as his paramount god much to the disappointment of the Jewish prophets who had expected him to acknowledge Yahweh as the one true God. He also allowed the Babylonian captives to resettle in their homelands and this has been confirmed by archaeological findings so at last there is some historical confirmation to go with the Bible narrative. The following is from Prof. Mark Throntveit (Lutheran Seminary) Period Exile:

"The history of Israel revolves around the double foci of exodus and exile. At the exodus, Israel began the process toward becoming a nation. The exile, however, signaled the loss of Israel's status as an independent nation, and even after the exile, Israel was merely a political backwater in the Persian province of Yehud. One would expect this to be a bleak period in the life of God's people: Jerusalem destroyed, the temple burned, the end of the Davidic dynasty, and the fruit and flower of the population deported. Yet, this was the most productive period of Israel's history; it fostered the birth of Judaism. The people came to recognize that God had not been defeated; indeed, God was the author of these events and could be worshiped apart from native land, temple, priest, or monarch. This was a crucial insight for Diaspora Judaism, those living in Babylon, Egypt, or elsewhere, deprived of their former institutions. Without a king, Israel remembered that Yahweh had always been their true king. A burned temple hundreds of miles away meant there were no sacrifices, but the Sabbath could become a time to worship and contemplate God's word in the synagogue. In fact, most of the Old Testament was written, compiled, or edited during the exile. Furthermore, circumcision came to be seen as a way to identify a people as easily as national boundaries.

The situation in Babylon is not well documented. Since most of the deportees refused to return to Jerusalem in 538 B.C.E., it seems safe to assume they enjoyed a measure of autonomy."

AUTHOR: <u>**Mark Throntveit, Professor of Hebrew and Old Testament**</u>

The Israelites escaped or were permitted to leave, the clutches of the Egyptians as a collection of tribes and proceeded to "The Promised Land". The general concensus, at least among sensible and open minded people is that the Tribes intermingled and integrated into the societies already in that land, nothing like the military escapades of the likes of Joshua, God would not have advocated such barbarism anyway, although there may have been smaller skirmishes along the way where the locals objected to these "foreigners" more or less taking over. As archaeological excavations continue to show, a great number of cities were already in ruins when the tribes arrived, the Tribes merely fixed things up. Can this be called the process of becoming a nation? The time period – Exodus out of Egypt circa 1500BC to the second major Exile circa 600BC would be the years that could be seen as pertaining to the building of the Israelite Nation but as has been noted there was so much dissent and disagreement during this that the Israelites were close to becoming masters of their own destruction. Nevertheless the world accepts that Israel existed as a nation of sorts but after the Exile this independent nation status was lost and isn't that the crux of the matter in the Middle East right up to the present?

The fact that Cyrus was so liberal in allowing Israel's worship of their one God was a tremendous help in maintaining Israel's place in history. This attitude was not the norm by any means and without Cyrus's influence there is some doubt that Israel would have survived, at the least the survival of the Jewish religion would have been set back hundreds of years. The following is a further extract from the Lutheran Seminary:

The end of Neo-Babylonian dominance made possible the return of the exiles to Judah and the restoration of their temple and community. Biblical texts (2 Chronicles 36:23; Ezra 1:2-4) corroborate the Persian policy of governing subject peoples in their own land and respecting the various deities worshiped in the empire. Not everyone, however, took advantage of this policy. Many chose to remain in Babylon, where Jewish scholarship eventually produced the Babylonian Talmud, the primary work of Jewish rabbinical interpretation (about 500 C.E.). Other Jews of the Diaspora, in what was to become Alexandria in Egypt during the Greek period, produced the Septuagint (the enormously influential Greek translation of the Old Testament) and the Apocrypha (found in Roman Catholic and Orthodox Bibles). The following is from Prof. Mark Throntveit:

"Those that did return to Judah found their homeland impoverished. Following the relocation of populations, political control was maintained through local governors whose primary task was to ensure the payment of royal taxes. The Persians also financed the restoration of temples, though the primary function of these institutions was the administration of Persian policy. Ezra 1 and 6 describe the rebuilding of the Jerusalem temple as mandated and financed by the Persian crown. Nehemiah's commission by the Persian king to rebuild the walls of Jerusalem indicates the strategic importance of the province to the empire (Nehemiah 1), as does the heavy tribute paid to Persia (Nehemiah 9:36-37). The prophets Haggai and Zechariah encouraged the people to rebuild the temple, promising that the "treasure of all the nations" would finance the project.

Significantly, the people were no longer defined politically and geographically, but ethnically and especially religiously. With the temple as the center of the restored community, the High Priest "ruled" in the absence of a king. The Jewish communities of Alexandria, Babylon, Elephantine, and elsewhere came to be known as the Diaspora and distinguished themselves from those who had not experienced exile, as did those who had remained in Judah. Both Judaism and Christianity would survive in a pluralistic world thanks to the lessons learned here.

During this time, the Pentateuch and much of the prophetic literature reached their final form. Chronicles, Ezra-Nehemiah, Haggai, Zechariah, Malachi, Isaiah 56-66, Job, parts of the Psalter and Proverbs, and perhaps Joel and Ecclesiastes were composed in this prolific period."

AUTHOR: <u>Mark Throntveit, Professor of Hebrew and Old Testament</u>

That Israel and the Jewish religion did survive is an amazing accomplishment and even since that time of hardship and captivity, the rest of the world has continued to persecute the Jews and attempt to establish different religions an adaptions and sects as if Judaism was lacking in something. Why is it not acceptable to all? Why change? Why was Jesus even introduced into the mix? But it seems there was dissent and disagreement even then amongst their own, this being the enmity that sprang up between the returning Jews and their northern neighbours in Samaria, the Samaritans. The Samaritans, although they viewed the resettlement of the Babylonian Jews with suspicion, had offered to help rebuild the Temple in Jerusalem. But the Yahwist priesthood had spurned their offer on the grounds that the Samaritans were no longer ethnically or theologically pure enough. This was the origin of the mutual hatred and contempt that is evident in the pages of the Old Testament and it would be five centuries before they would be rehabilitated in the parable of the Good Samaritan. During those five hundred years the Samaritans went their own separate way and to this day they are still a people apart, strictly speaking considered neither Jew nor Gentile but a people who claim to be the true descendants of Israel with their own archaic version of the Pentateuch and their own uncompromising observance of the laws of Moses. The point being that even here, so close to achieving their goal of monotheism, the worship of the one true God, they still cannot get it all together. What hope for the future?

Although the Jerusalem Temple had been restored by 515 BC, Jerusalem itself remained an insignificant part of an insignificant Persian province. But in 445 BC things changed with the arrival in Jerusalem of a special governor for Judah, a man called Nehemiah. Nehemiah was a high ranking Jewish official in the court of the Persian king, Artaxerxes I and he persuaded the king to allow the rebuilding of the walls and he was sent to Jerusalem with special powers to get this done. Excavations have shown what a terrible state of ruin the walls and terraces had fallen into after the destruction of the city by Nebuchadnezzar but Nehemiah completed the tremendous project of rebuilding the walls of

Jerusalem in only fifty-two days and within these new city walls there was ensconced a population of some 10,000 people, it is thought - most of them descendants of exiles returned from Babylon. Jerusalem itself, as a community, was rebuilt at last and The Exile, at last was really over.

8
GREEK RULE
400 BC to 200 BC

The following paragraph is a portion of chapter 12 "Archaeology of the Bible" by Magnus Magnusson:

"In the Old Testament, history ended with the return to Jerusalem under Persian patronage but history went on its own way nonetheless. History was still to have a major impact on the Middle East, starting with one of the most remarkable young men who ever lived - Alexander the Great of Macedonia. In ten brief years, from 334 to 323 BC, he conquered the known world. He destroyed the Persians and took over their empire – and that meant he took over the whole Middle East."

In the period from about 500 BC, after the temple had been restored to about 340 BC, just prior to Greek rule, what had happened in Judah as far as the Jewish religion is concerned? It appears there was not much leadership from the priests and because there was no king it fell upon the prophets to try and instil in the people the words of God and remind them that God was still with them despite all that had happened. Some of the priests resented the prophets' influence but eventually it was the priests who were instrumental in bringing the nation together again. Not just a nation of people but the formation of Jewish religion associated with that nation. Because there had been such a mixture of Jews, gentiles and others returning to Judah and Jerusalem and in fact many inter- marriages resulting in children who knew nothing of the Hebrew history, it was a task but there were many conversions. The term 'prophet' in the Old Testament means a representative of God whose duties were to explain current philosophies and preach the word of God and not to forecast future events as we understand 'prophet' to mean. The prophet Jeremiah recognized that change was needed from the old written words and ways and in effect told the people to stop worrying about the old Ark of the Covenant (which may have been taken to Egypt, no one knows for certain) and they did not need this form of altar to worship God but worship of God needed to come from the heart and in fact Jeremiah introduced a 'New Covenant'. So even though the period just prior to Greek rule found the Jews still under Persian rule, they had flourished and grown as a nation and as a religion. Not sure what the physical boundaries of that nation were but as far as Alexander the Great was concerned that didn't really matter.

Paragraph excerpt from "Archaeology of the Bible" by Magnus Magnusson:

"This was the first time that Europe, Western civilization as such, had ever annexed the Near and Middle East and the effect was massive and enduring. It introduced to the ancient Orient a new way of living and thinking called Hellenism The impact of Hellenism on Judaism is hard to assess" but obviously there was a crisis of faith and a challenge by the moral individualism of the Helenistic way of thinking.

Alexander was not a pagan because Aristotle was not a pagan. Aristotle's concept of God was that a Creator exists. Alexander had been tutored by Aristotle. The Greek philosopher referred to God as the 'First Cause.' He pushed the button, so to speak. However, once He did so He did not do anything more. What happened on Earth did not interest him. Therefore, there was no interference from Heaven as to what happened on Earth. It was another way of unburdening themselves of conscience – except now with the stamp of belief in God.

Nevertheless, the Greeks believed that God existed, which is very important because it will help explain one reason why Alexander was able to tolerate the Jewish religion, whereas many of the Persian emperors were not. Aristotle knew that all the stories of the gods – from Apollo to Zeus – were made-up. Alexander, as Aristotle's student, also believed that. Thanks to Aristotle, therefore, the ideas of the Jews were much more acceptable to Alexander. One of Alexander's campaigns brought him to the Land of Israel. He arrived during the reign of the great High Priest, the last of the Men of the Great Assembly, Simon the Just. Most historians say that he came in about the year 329 BC. (He was dead by 323 BC.)

The Jews were terrified of the now victorious Greeks, because they had backed Persia in the war. There were two choices. This story will be repeated over and over again in the time of the Second Temple. One was to fight, which is what the Jews did later with the Romans. The second was to somehow come to an accommodation with the enemy.

Simon the Just chose the second course. The Jews were not about to defeat Alexander in battle; therefore, the correct way to deal with the matter was to come to an accommodation with him. Because of Aristotle, Alexander was positively disposed toward the Jews. Instead of destroying and subjugating them, he made an arrangement with them. As long as they would be his loyal vassals and pay their taxes they could remain autonomous. That was an enormous concession because Alexander was rarely that accommodating to anyone. Alexander did not plan to die at an early age, but his death left the world in chaos. The man who had controlled it was suddenly not there.

His entire empire could have fallen apart at that moment, but split into two – governed by two of Alexander's generals. The northern empire was ruled by Seleucus and became known as the Seleucid Dynasty. He was headquartered in the city that is today Damascus. The southern empire was ruled by Ptolemy and was headquartered in the city of Alexandria, which had been renamed in honor of Alexander.

The two generals agreed upon virtually everything — except the line that divided the northern empire from the southern. That put the Land of Israel smack in the middle of their disagreement. The Jews were caught in this tremendous power struggle. The story of the next 130 years would be the balancing act of the Jewish people between the two giants. Sometimes the Jews teetered to the south and sometimes to the north. The south attempted to win the Jewish people by persuasion and culture. The north attempted to do so by force. Both would fail. Like all others in the region, the Jews bitterly resented the Greeks. They were more foreign than any group they had ever seen. In a state founded on maintaining the purity of the Hebrew religion, the gods of the Greeks seemed wildly offensive. In a society rigidly opposed to the exposure of the body, the Greek practice of wrestling in the nude and deliberately dressing light must have been appalling! In a religion that specifically singles out homosexuality as a crime against Yahweh, the Greek attitude and even preference for homosexuality must have been incomprehensible.

In general, though, the Greeks left the Jews alone; adopting Cyrus's policy, they allowed the Jews to run their own country, declared that the law of Judah was the Torah, and attempted to preserve Jewish religion but when the Seleucid king, Antiochus IV, desecrated the Temple in 168 BC, he touched off a Jewish revolt under the Maccabees; for a brief time, Judah became an independent state again. During this period, Jewish history takes place in several areas: in Judah, in Mesopotamia and other parts of the Middle East, and Egypt. For the dispersion of the Jews had begun during the Exile, and large, powerful groups of Jews lived all throughout the Persian Empire and later the Hellenistic kingdoms ("Hellenistic"="Greek"). The Greeks brought with them a brand new concept: the "polis," or "city-state." Among the revolutionary ideas of the "polis" was the idea of naturalization. In the ancient world, it was not possible to become a citizen of a state if you weren't born in that state. If you were born in Israel, and you moved to Tyre, or Babylon, or Egypt, you were always an Israelite. Your legal status in the country you're living in would be "foreigner" or "sojourner." The Greeks, however, would allow foreigners to become citizens in the polis - it became possible all throughout the Middle East for Hebrews and others to become citizens of states other than Judah. This is vital for understanding the Jewish dispersion; for the rights of citizenship (or near-citizenship, called polituemata) allowed Jews to remain outside of Judaea and still thrive. In many foreign cities throughout the Hellenistic world, the Jews formed unified and solid communities; Jewish women enjoyed more rights and autonomy in these communities rather than at home.

The most important event of the Hellenistic period, though, is the translation of the Torah into Greek in Ptolemaic Egypt. The Greeks, in fact, were somewhat interested (not much) in the Jewish religion, but it seems that they wanted a copy of the Jewish scriptures for the library at Alexandria. During the Exile, the Exiles began to purify their religion and practices and turned to the Mosaic books as their model. After the Exile, the Torah became the authoritative code of the Jews, recognized first by Persia and later by the Greeks as the Hebrew "law." In 458 BC, Artaxerxes I of Persia made the Torah the "law of the Judaean king."

So the Greeks wanted a copy and set about translating it. Called the **Septuagint** after the number of translators it required ("septuaginta" is Greek for "seventy"), the text is far from perfect. The Hebrew Torah had not settled down into a definitive version, and a number of mistranslations creep in for reasons ranging from political expediency to confusion. For instance, the Hebrew Torah is ruthlessly anti-Egyptian; after all, the founding event of the Hebrew people was the oppression of the Hebrews by the Egyptians and the delivery from Egypt. The Septuagint translators—who are, after all, working for the Greek rulers of Egypt—go about effacing much of the anti-Egyptian aspects. On the other hand, there are words they can't translate into Greek, such as "berit," which they translate "diatheke," or "promise" (in Latin and English, the word is incorrectly translated "covenant"). These interpretations or mistranslations have been commented on earlier and have resulted in numerous unnecessary conflicts throughout history.

Despite these imperfections, the Septuagint is a watershed in Jewish history. More than any other event in Jewish history, this translation would make the Hebrew religion into a world religion. It would otherwise have faded from memory like the infinity of Semitic religions that have been lost to us. This Greek version made the Hebrew Scriptures available to the Mediterranean world and to early Christians who were otherwise fain to regard Christianity as a religion unrelated to Judaism. Even with a Greek translation, the Hebrew Scriptures came within a hair's breadth of being tossed out of the Christian canon. From this Greek translation, the Hebrew view of God, of history, of law, and of the human condition, in all its magnificence would spread around the world. The dispersion, or Diaspora, of the Jews would involve ideas as well as people.

9

ROMAN RULE AND CHRISTIANITY
200 BC to 200 AD

Schism – A division in religion. Was not the first schism the doctrine of Jesus Christ? What was wrong with Abraham's take on God's work as it had been for almost 2000 years?

In 332 BC., Alexander the Great of Macedon destroyed the Persian Empire but largely ignored Judah. After Alexander's death, his generals divided--and subsequently fought over--his empire. In 301 B.C., Ptolemy I took direct control of the Jewish homeland, but he made no serious effort to interfere in its religious affairs. Ptolemy's successors were in turn supplanted by the Seleucids, and in 175 B.C. Antiochus IV seized power. He launched a campaign to crush Judaism, and in 167 B.C. he sacked the Temple.

The violation of the Second Temple, which had been built about 520-515 B.C., provoked a successful Jewish rebellion under the generalship of Judas (Judah) Maccabaeus. In 140 B.C. the Hasmonean Dynasty began under the leadership of Simon Maccabaeus, who served as ruler, high priest, and commander in chief. Simon, who was assassinated a few years later, formalized what Judas had begun, the establishment of a theocracy, something not found in any biblical text.

Despite priestly rule, Jewish society became Hellenized except in its generally staunch adherence to monotheism. Although rural life was relatively unchanged, cities such as Jerusalem rapidly adopted the Greek language, sponsored games and sports, and in more subtle ways adopted and absorbed the culture of the Hellenes. Even the high priests bore such names as Jason and Menelaus. Biblical scholars have identified extensive Greek influence in the drafting of commentaries and interpolations of ancient texts during and after the Greek period. The most obvious influence of the Hellenistic period can be discerned in the early literature of the new faith, Christianity.

Halliday, Fred, 100 myths about the Middle East

The historical truth of the life of Jesus Christ is based on the four Gospels.

"The authority of Christianity as a 'world' religion rests on the claim that a historic personage, Jesus Christ, was born around 0 AD in Palestine, preached the doctrine we now call 'Christianity' and died on the Cross around 33 AD. However, on the basis of conventional historiographic criteria, the evidence for the historical Christ is weak. There is no archaeological evidence of any kind that would support this claim. The main literary sources, the four Gospels, are of Christian origin, and so suspect, as well as written well after the events described. The first of the four canonical gospels to be written, that of Mark, was written in Rome about 65 AD, three decades after the death of Christ; that of Luke in Syria, some time after 65 AD; that of Matthew, in Palestine between 75 and 90 AD; and that of Iohn, in Asia Minor between 90 and 100 AD. The first non- Christian source to mention Jesus "was the historian Flavius Josephus, who mentions the martyrdom of James, 'brother of Jesus, known as Christ', although another passage in Iosephus, who mentioning Christ is thought by some scholars to have been tampered with by Christian scribes."

Jesus Christ - myth or reality? – Again, no records or confirmation of his existence except as recorded in the Bible. Was he, (if he existed) another prophet, as per the likes of Isaiah and Jeremiah? Remember there was an abundance of them in The Old Testament. He certainly would have been a Jew and familiar with the Jewish Scriptures of the time and if he was a serious follower of the Jewish faith then his disgust at the behavior of the temple priests in Jerusalem would have been understandable and his outspoken criticism of money lending and absolute corruption of all that he believed in, going on right there in the Holiest of places would have come to the attention of the Roman authorities. Was this sufficient reason for his arrest and subsequent execution? Did the Romans actually believe that this man was a threat to their rule? Was Jesus an activist in the eyes of the Romans? Was it because the Jews had strayed way too far from the original Abrahamic teachings and it was probably better to start anew? Was there too much violence associated with those original teachings and was it time for a more peaceable approach? This would be a commendable reason and certainly Christianity began as a peaceful doctrine but that is not how it stayed as history will show.

Under the Hasmonean Dynasty, Judah became comparable in extent and power to the ancient Davidic dominion. Internal political and religious discord ran high, however, especially between the Pharisees, who interpreted the written law by adding a wealth of oral law, and the Sadducees, an aristocratic priestly class who called for strict adherence to the written law. In 64 BC., dynastic contenders for the throne appealed for support to Pompey, who was then establishing Roman power in Asia. The next year Roman legions seized Jerusalem, and Pompey installed one of the contenders for the throne as high priest, but without the title of king. Eighty years of independent Jewish sovereignty ended, and the period of Roman dominion began.

In the subsequent period of Roman wars, Herod was confirmed by the Roman Senate as king of Judah in 37 BC. and reigned until his death in 4 BC. Nominally independent, Judah was actually in bondage to Rome, and the land was formally annexed in 6 BC. as part of the province of Syria Palestina. Rome did, however, grant the Jews religious autonomy and some judicial and legislative rights through the Sanhedrin. The Sanhedrin, which traces its origins to a council of elders established under Persian rule (333 BC. to 165 BC.) was the highest Jewish legal and religious body under Rome. The Great Sanhedrin, located on the Temple Mount in Jerusalem, supervised smaller local Sanhedrins and was the final authority on many important religious, political, and legal issues, such as declaring war, trying a high priest, and supervising certain rituals. Scholars have sharply debated the structure and composition of the Sanhedrin. The Jewish historian Josephus and the New Testament present the Sanhedrin as a political and judicial council whereas the Talmud describes it as a religious, legislative body headed by a court of seventy-one sages. Another view holds that there were two separate Sanhedrins. The political Sanhedrin was composed primarily of the priestly Sadducee aristocracy and was charged by the Roman procurator with responsibility for civil order, specifically in matters involving imperial directives. The religious Sanhedrin of the Pharisees was concerned with religious law and doctrine, which the Romans disregarded as long as civil order was not threatened. Foremost among the Pharisee leaders of the time were the noted teachers, Hillel and Shammai.

Jesus Christ enters the fray:

Jesus was born in the Roman world into a Jewish home but of course the vast majority of persons living in the Roman Empire at that time were pagans or polytheists with beliefs in many gods. Judaism, the religion of Jesus, was distinct in the ancient world for worshipping only one god but Jews made up only a very small portion of the Roman Empire, maybe around seven percent so a new religion such as Christianity would seem to have very little chance of becoming established. In fact there were a wide range of Judaisms with some not being completely monolithic and possibly this fact along with other temple activity concerns convinced Jesus to become alienated with his early learnings of the Jewish faith.

Christianity originated with Jesus of Nazareth, and began as a sect within Judaism. It was originally composed of Jewish followers and seemed to appeal especially to the poorer classes. His disciples were simple people, some were fishermen from accounts in the Bible but there is a major difficulty in reconstructing his life because there are no references to him in any Roman, Greek or other similar sources throughout the first century. Josephus is the only one non-Christian Jewish source to mention him, and that only briefly. As a result the only accounts available are by his own followers which are contained in the New Testament and even these accounts are contradictory.

Jesus came to believe he was the Son of God and his teachings were largely about the coming Kingdom of God and the need to prepare for it and it was these teachings that roused suspicion among the upper classes and the leaders of the Jewish religion. These helped persuade the Roman governor, already concerned about unrest among the Jews, that Jesus was a dangerous agitator. Jesus was put to death as a result, crucified like a common criminal, about 30 AD. His followers believed that he was resurrected on the third day after his death, a proof that he was the Son of God. This belief helped the religion spread farther among Jewish communities in the Middle East, both within the Roman Empire and beyond. As they realized that the Messiah was not immediately returning to earth to set up the Kingdom of God, the disciples of Jesus began to fan out, particularly around the eastern Mediterranean, to spread the new Christian message.

Gradually over the next 250 years, Christianity won a growing number of converts. By the 4th century A.D., about 10 percent of the residents of the Roman Empire were Christian, and the new religion had also made converts elsewhere in the Middle East and Ethiopia. With its particularly great appeal to some of the poor, Christianity was well positioned to reflect social grievances amongst slaves, dispossessed farmers and city dwellers lacking means of support who found hope in a religion that promised rewards after death. Christianity also answered cultural and spiritual needs - especially but not exclusively among the poor - left untended by mainstream Roman religion and culture. Roman values were of a materialistic nature and they did not join peoples of the empire in spiritual loyalties whereas Christianity had a certain appeal. As the empire consolidated, reducing direct political participation, a number of mystery religions spread from the Middle East and Egypt, religions that offered emotionally charged rituals. Christianity, though far more than a mystery religion, had some of these qualities and won converts on this basis as well. Christianity, in sum, gained ground in part because of features of Roman political and cultural life.

The spread of Christianity also benefited from some of the positive qualities of Rome's great empire. Political stability and communications over a wide area aided missionary efforts, while the Roman example helped inspire the government forms of the growing Christian church.

Early Christian communities regulated themselves, but with expansion more formal government was introduced, with bishops playing a role not unlike Rome's provincial governors. Bishops headed churches in regional centers and supervised the activities of other churches in the area. Bishops in politically powerful cities, including Rome, gained particular authority. Roman principles also helped move what initially had been a religion among Jews to a genuinely cosmopolitan stance. Under the leadership of Paul, converted to Christianity about A.D. 35, Christian missionaries began to move away from insistence that adherents of the new religion must follow Jewish law. Rather, in the spirit of Rome and of Hellenism, the new faith was seen as universal, open to all whether or not they followed Jewish practices in diet, male circumcision, and so on. Paul's conversion to Christianity proved vital as he was Jewish, but he had been born in a Greek city and was familiar with Greco-Roman culture. He helped explain basic Christian beliefs in terms other adherents of this culture could grasp and it was Paul's stress on Christianity as a universal religion, requiring abandonment of other religious beliefs, and his related use of Greek - the dominant language of the day throughout the eastern Mediterranean - that particularly transformed the new faith.

Adherents of the new religion clashed with Roman authorities, to be sure. Christians, who put their duties to God first, would not honor the emperor as a divinity and might seem to reject the authority of the state in other spheres. Several early emperors, including the mad Nero, persecuted

Christians, killing some and driving their worship underground. Persecution was not constant, however, which helps explain why the religion continued to spread. It resumed only in the 4th century, when several emperors sought to use religious conformity and new claims to divinity as a way of cementing loyalties to a declining state.

Christianity had more to do with opening a new era in the history of the Mediterranean region than with shaping the later Roman Empire. Yet important connections did exist that explain features of Christianity and of later Roman history. Though not a Roman product and though benefiting in part from the empire's decline, Christianity in some of its qualities can be counted as part of the Greco-Roman legacy.

So there it is – a reason for Christianity – the early stages of the religion focused on cleansing the Jewish religion of stiff rituals and haughty leaders. It had little at first to do with Roman culture. Already there were three major sects within Judaism in the Second Temple period, the Pharisees, the Sadducees and the Essenes who aroused public interest later on with the discovery of the Dead Sea Scrolls. All of the people cannot be pleased all of the time, there is never a more suitable saying than that regarding religion!

Chafing under foreign rule, a Jewish nationalist movement of the fanatical sect known as the Zealots challenged Roman control in A.D. 66. After a protracted siege begun by Vespasian, the Roman commander in Judah, but completed under his son Titus in A.D. 70, Jerusalem and the Second Temple were seized and destroyed by the Roman legions. The last Zealot survivors perished in A.D. 73 at the mountain fortress of Massada, about fifty-six kilometers southwest of Jerusalem above the western shore of the Dead Sea.

During the siege of Jerusalem, Rabbi Yohanan Ben-Zakki received Vespasian's permission to withdraw to the town of Yibna (also seen as Jabneh) on the coastal plain, about twenty-four kilometers southwest of present-day Tel Aviv. There an academic center or academy was set up and became the central religious authority; its jurisdiction was recognized by Jews in Palestine and beyond. Roman rule, nevertheless, continued. Emperor Hadrian (A.D. 117-38) endeavored to establish cultural uniformity and issued several repressive edicts, including one against circumcision.

The edicts sparked the Bar-Kochba Rebellion of 135 BC, which was crushed by the Romans. Hadrian then closed the Academy at Yibna, and prohibited both the study of the Torah and the observance of the Jewish way of life derived from it. Judah was included in Syria Palestina, Jerusalem was renamed Aelia Capitolina, and Jews were forbidden to come within sight of the city. Once a year on the anniversary of the destruction of the Temple, controlled entry was permitted, allowing Jews to mourn at a remaining fragment on the Temple site, the Western Wall, which became known as the Wailing Wall. The Diaspora, which had begun with the Babylonian captivity in the sixth century BC and which had resumed early in the Hellenistic period, now involved most Jews in an exodus from what they continued to view as the land promised to them as the descendants of Abraham.

Following the destruction of the Temple in 70 A.D., and especially after the suppression of the Bar-Kochba Rebellion in 135 A.D., religio-nationalist aspects of Judaism were supplanted by a growing intellectual-spiritual trend. Lacking a state, the survival of the Jewish people was dependent on study and observance of the written law, the Torah. To maintain the integrity and cohesiveness of the community, the Torah was enlarged into a coherent system of moral theology and community law. The rabbi and the synagogue became the normative institutions of Judaism, which thereafter was essentially a congregationalist faith.

The focus on study led to the compilation of the Talmud, an immense commentary on the Torah that thoroughly analyzed the application of Jewish law to the day-to-day life of the Jewish community. The complexity of argument and analysis contained in the Palestinian Talmud (100-425 A.D.) and the more authoritative Babylonian Talmud (completed around 500) reflected the high level of intellectual maturity attained by the various schools of Jewish learning. This inward-looking intellectualism, along with a rigid adherence to the laws and rituals of Judaism, maintained the separateness of the Jewish people, enabling them to survive the exilic experience despite the lure of conversion and frequent outbreaks of anti-Semitism.

The final Jewish revolt against Rome in AD 135 signaled the beginning of the end of the Hebrew language, until around AD 500 a group of Jewish scholars known as Masoretes of Tiberius began to preserve the Bible in the Hebrew language.

From the end of the first century to the fourth century, scribes copied and translated manuscripts in various languages.

If there ever was a time for errors, omissions and opinions to creep in, this was it.

10
BYZANTINE RULE AND THE PERSIAN INVASION
200 AD to 600 AD

By the end of the 4th century, following Emperor Constantine's adoption of Christianity (313) and the founding of the Byzantine Empire, the Land of Israel had become a predominantly Christian country. Churches were built on Christian holy sites in Jerusalem, Bethlehem and Galilee, and monasteries were established in many parts of the country. The Jews were deprived of their former relative autonomy, as well as of their right to hold public positions, and were forbidden to enter Jerusalem except on one day of the year (Tisha b'Av - ninth of Av) to mourn the destruction of the Temple.

The small group of Jesus' followers that gathered in Jerusalem after his departure did not call themselves anything. The word Christian came into use years later and was at first a derogatory term applied by outsiders. When the books of the New Testament were written, the word used to name the believers was simply assembly. It is now the most common term applied to groups of Christians as well as to the totality of the world's Christian membership. The word is also frequently applied to denominations, a usage now so common as to be unavoidable. Denominations are, however, institutional arrangements based on specific viewpoints and traditional practices. They exist as a result of long historical development, doctrinal diversity, and geographical separation. Specific viewpoints based on an individual's interpretation could mean an endless list of denominations or sects – hasn't this only added to "religious confusion"?

The early Christians were all Jews. They differed from their fellow Jews only in that they believed that the Messiah had come. Had they remained quiet about their conviction, they might well have remained a sect within Judaism. However, they insisted on preaching to all who would listen that the Jesus whom the Jewish authorities had persecuted was the one Israel had long awaited. History would certainly have been re-written had they remained quiet, but the separation of the two camps was perhaps due to Paul's assertion that Christians did not have to become Jews, they did not have to be subjected to all the rites, rituals and laws of Israel's religion and this fact in itself aroused intense hostility of the Jews.

The Persian invasion of 614 led by Heraclius was welcomed and aided by the Jews, who were inspired by messianic hopes of deliverance. In gratitude for their help, they were granted the administration of Jerusalem, an interlude which lasted about three years. Subsequently, the Byzantine army regained the city (629) and again expelled its Jewish population.

The precarious balance of power between Persia and Byzantine persisted till the early sixth century when the sovereigns of these two empires, threatened by other enemies, began a correspondence that was meant to secure the frontier between them. The Byzantine Emperor Maurice and the Persian Khosrow II Parviz (the "Victorious") finally signed an "eternal" peace accord which was to last for ten years. In 602 a soldier's mutiny overthrew the Byzantine monarch and placed a junior officer named Phocas on the throne.

Khosrow seized this opportunity to renew the war, leading the Persian armies into Byzantine territories in the Near East. In 613 his soldiers completed the conquest of Syria and captured Damascus. As the Persian armies were advancing, Jewish communities were rising in revolt against local Byzantine rulers and hailing Persians as liberators.

In the early summer of 614, Khosrow's troops entered Jerusalem and massacred its Christian population. The role of the Jews during this Persian siege and conquest of Jerusalem remains unclear. Later Christian sources, however, accused the community of collaboration with the invaders and of destruction of many churches in the city.

On the other hand, there is clear evidence that the status of the Jewish population under Persian rule had deteriorated prior to 617. The Persians apparently realized that there was little to be gained from appeasing a small local minority. According to contemporary Jewish documents, a Jewish leader by the name of Nehemiah ben Hushi'el, probably a messianic figure, was executed: "And there was trouble in Israel as never before" (Book of Zerubbabel).

The Persian victory, however, was not to last. Following a victory in Nineveh in 627, the Byzantine Emperor Heraclius besieged the Persian capital of Ctesiphon. Khosrow was deposed and assassinated, and his son, who wished to end the war, died in 629. Heraclius reached an agreement with the Persian army commander who ordered his troops to withdraw from Mesopotamia, Egypt, Syria and Palestine, and also returned to the Byzantines the relics of the True Cross. On March 29, 629, as Heraclius triumphantly entered Jerusalem, Christians wept with joy at the miracle of the restoration of the True Cross. In his hour of glory, the emperor magnanimously refrained from taking reprisal against the Jews.

Stepping back in time a little to the first century AD it has already been noted that three major sects within Judaism had already arisen – the Pharisees, the Sadducees and the Essenes and this recurring fact of separation from the original is the basis of one of the two main themes of this book, the other being the association of violence with religion. The reasons for the formation of these sects are too complicated for the scope of this book and probably too complicated for the writer to comprehend but it is obviously a problem in itself that people have been unable to accept the original concepts and as history will show it has had a direct effect on historical conflict of the worst magnitude.

After Jesus Christ's crucifixion his followers, called Christians, scattered to spread the word or maybe because they figured they may be next. Guilt by association so to speak. Christianity, then, can be called a sect of Judaism, the main difference and a great concern among most of the leading Jews was that the followers of Jesus Christ believed that Jesus was the Messiah. This fact seems straightforward enough but already in the early years of Christianity there was appearing another division or separation within the Christian assembly, the interpretation of Roman Catholicism is closely related to the interpretation of Christianity (here is that word again – 'interpretation'). For by its own reading of history, Roman Catholicism began with the very beginnings of the Christian movement, an essential component of the definition of any one of the other branches of Christendom. So there began a movement to transform the primitive Christian movement into a church that was recognizably "catholic," namely, a church that had begun to possess identifiable norms of doctrine and life, fixed structures of church authority, and, at least in principle, a universality (which is what "catholic" meant) that extended to all of humanity. Again, why could there not have been some acceptance of what already was? Indeed if the new Catholic sect could have foreseen what the future held in terms of deaths caused, non-believers tortured and atrocities committed in the name of the Catholic Church they would have had second thoughts. The following paragraphs are from Religious Facts.com and as such are offered simply for opinion and discussion:

What is the Catholic Religion? The following Catholic references are taken from Religious Facts.com and my comment here serves as a disclaimer on Religious Facts behalf. However, I do believe the commentary is correct.

"For the first thousand years of Christianity there was no "Roman Catholicism" as we know it today, simply because there was no Eastern Orthodoxy or Protestantism to distinguish it. There was only the "one, holy, catholic church" affirmed by the early creeds, which was the body of Christian believers all over the world, united by common traditions, beliefs, church structure and worship (catholic simply means "universal"). Thus, throughout the Middle Ages, if you were a Christian, you belonged to the Catholic Church. Any Christianity other than the Catholic Church was a heresy, not a denomination.

History of Catholicism

Roman Catholicism traces its history to the apostles, especially the Apostle Peter. St. Peter is considered the first pope, and every pope since him is regarded as his spiritual successor. This gives the leader of the church spiritual authority and provides a means for resolving disputes that could divide the church. Through trials like persecution, heresy, and the Reformation, the notion that the church leadership represents the continuation of an unbroken line from the apostles and their teachings ("apostolic succession") has contributed to the survival of Christianity.

The Catholic Pope

However, the idea of the "pope" did not exist from the beginning of the church. It was not until several centuries after Christ that the church began to develop into the "Roman Catholic Church" as we think of it today, with its particular doctrines, practices, and hierarchical system of authority. Thus Catholics and non-Catholics alike are able to claim they are most faithful to the message of the apostles and the early church. From the Catholic perspective, the early church is faithfully continued in the developments of later centuries, while non-Catholics tend to regard the church as having corrupted the original message of Christianity.

In the years of persecution prior to the Emperor's conversion, the church was focused primarily on survival. There were prominent church leaders whose authority was recognized - primarily those who had known the apostles - but no central authority.

But with the conversion of Emperor Constantine in 318 AD, the church began to adopt a governmental structure mirroring that of the Empire, in which geographical provinces were ruled by bishops based in the major city of the area. Soon, the bishops of major cities in the empire emerged as preeminent, including the bishops of Jerusalem, Alexandria,

Antioch, Rome, and Constantinople. It was natural that Rome would eventually become the most important of these. It was not only the capital of the empire, but the city in which the apostles Peter and Paul were believed to have been martyred.

The Roman bishop Leo I (440-461) is considered the first pope by historians, as he was the first to claim ultimate authority over all of Christendom. In his writings one can find all the traditional arguments for papal authority, most notably that which asserts Christ had designated Peter and his successors the "rock" on which the church would be built.

Leo's claims were strengthened greatly by his own impressive career as Bishop of Rome. In 445 he earned the express support of Emperor Valentian, who said the Bishop of Rome was the law for all. In 451, he called the important Council of Chalcedon, which put to rest Christological issues that had been plaguing the church. In 452, he impressively saved Rome from Attila the Hun. It is said that the Pope met the warrior at the gates and somehow persuaded him to spare the city. Legend has it that Attila saw Peter and Paul marching along with Leo to defend their city. In 455 he was not as successful with Vandal invaders, but led negotiations with them and succeeded in preventing the burning of Rome (it was, however, plundered)."

With the fourth century came St. Jerome and he was far ahead of his time. At this time in history there was mass confusion surrounding the variety and number of biblical manuscripts and Jerome, being a master of biblical Hebrew and Greek translated the Bible into Latin.

Which manuscript did he decide to translate from, one wonders?

Not only did he standardize the text but his Bible became the official Latin version of the Roman Catholic Church. This edition would later be called the *Vulgate* which simply means "the published version".

But even this masterpiece in translation did not suit some of the powers that be, at that point in time.

This interpretation and translation of various manuscripts and so called scholars editing to suit their own take on things has been a huge cause of confusion to the world of religion and this interference continues throughout history. Surely the basic "Do you believe in God" and attempting to live by "The Ten commandments" is all that's required? What's with all the man-made mumbo-Jumbo that's crammed into us from an early age?

11
ARAB RULE – THE
SPREAD OF ISLAM
600 AD to 1000 AD

In 602, the two world powers were the Christian Byzantine Empire and the Zoroastrian (fire worshipping) Persian Empire. That year, Khosroe II of Persia attacked the Byzantine Empire, capturing huge swathes of their territories including the Middle East, Eastern Europe, and Egypt.

Some historians define the Christian counteroffensive against Persia as the first Crusade. To finance the war, they stripped metal and bronze from monuments and even from the Hagia Sophia, the most important church of the capital (nowadays a prominent mosque and Istanbul's most famous landmark). Towards the end of the campaign, his armies even surged up to the walls of Constantinople, capital of the Byzantine kingdom. In the end, Khosroe was thwarted by the Byzantine leader Heraclius, one of the greatest military geniuses of history. Although both empires survived intact, years of war left them too weak to withstand the Muslim juggernaut that rolled in afterwards.

Many think that a religion starts with its main figure and very often we see that many religions get names after those important religious personas. Christianity was named after Jesus Christ, Buddhism after Buddha, etc. Very few religions carry the name independent of its "founder" and one of those is Islam. For Muslims, Islam did not begin with Prophet Muhammad but has existed since the time humanity came into being.

Islam is one of the Abrahamic family of faiths that also includes Judaism and Christianity. Muslims recognize Abraham, Moses, Jesus and other Biblical figures as part of this tradition.

Muhammad was born in the year 570 AD in Mecca. Muslims believe that, when he was 40, the angel Gabriel appeared to him in a cave where he was meditating, and, over the next 23 years, revealed to him messages from God. These messages were compiled into the Qur'an. Muslims do not regard Muhammad as divine with God, but as the last of the prophets. Muslims believe that the prophets of the Hebrew Scriptures and Jesus were true prophets, but in Muhammad the prophetic tradition was perfected and Islam was to be the true religion of Abraham and the Bible.

The Islamic holy book, the Qur'an or Koran, was allegedly revealed to Muhammad by Allah over a 23-year period, beginning in 610 AD. Muhammad would recite these revelations and his followers would write those utterances down. In it we learn that Allah is the creator and sustainer of the world. In Mecca, not all were prepared to embrace this new monotheistic religion of Islam as demonstrated by Muhammad. The most powerful tribe at that time was the Quaraish led by Abu Jahl and this confrontation led to Muhammad and his followers leaving Mecca and establishing the first Islamic community at Medina in 622 AD. Reasonably peaceful at this point. Around 624 AD, Muhammad broke with his Jewish supporters because they refused to recognize him as a prophet and adopt Islam, so he banished or executed all of them. In this same year Muhammad and his followers defeated an army from Mecca and his chief rival in Mecca, Abu Jahl was executed. Already the violence! Not just violence but butchery and a lot more to come. How can this be justified as religion? A power hungry thug destroying everything in his path that he doesn't agree with and convincing other similar yahoos that it is God's wish. Though according to the Muslim historical tradition, the majority of non-Muslim peoples of the Old World, not desiring to submit to Islam or its laws (Sharia), fought back, though most were eventually defeated and subsumed. Nonetheless the string of atrocities attributed to this self-proclaimed 'prophet' is quite unbelievable and for any who doubt this need only to pick up a history book.

Muhammad died of a fever in 632 at the age of 63, with his violent religion spread over most of Arabia. His method of forcing others to convert under duress had several negative consequences, beginning with the civil wars that were immediately engaged in following his death. Many tribes wanted out of Islam and had to be kept in the empire via horrific violence.

Abu Sufyan, the Meccan leader who was literally forced to "embrace" Islam at the point of a sword actually had the last laugh. He skillfully worked his own family into the line of succession and his son, Muawiya, became the heir to Muhammad's empire at the expense of the prophet's own family. In fact, Abu Sufyan almost lived to witness his son and grandson kill off Muhammad's own grandchildren and assume control of the Islamic empire.

Muhammad's failure to leave a clear successor resulted in a deep schism that quickly devolved into violence and persists to this day as the Sunni/ Shia conflict. His own family fell apart and literally went to war with each other in the first few years. Thousands of Muslims were killed fighting each other in a battle between Muhammad's favorite wife, Aisha, and his adopted son, Ali.

Infidels fared no better. Through Muhammad's teachings and example, his followers viewed worldly life as a constant physical battle between the House of Peace (Dar al-Salaam) and the House of War (Dar al-Harb). Muslims are instructed to invite their enemies to either embrace Islam, pay jizya (protection money), or die.

The original split between Sunnis and Shia occurred soon after the death of the Prophet Muhammad, in the year 632. "There was a dispute in the community of Muslims in present-day Saudi Arabia over the question of succession," says Augustus Norton, author of Hezbollah: A Short History. "That is to say, who is the rightful successor to the Prophet?"

Most of the Prophet Muhammad's followers wanted the community of Muslims to determine who would succeed him. A smaller group thought that someone from his family should take up his mantle. They favored Ali, who was married to Muhammad's daughter, Fatimah.

"Shia believed that leadership should stay within the family of the Prophet," notes Gregory Gause, professor of Middle East politics at the University of Vermont. "And thus they were the partisans of Ali, his cousin and son-in-law. Sunnis believed that leadership should fall to the person who was deemed by the elite of the community to be best able to lead the community. And it was fundamentally that political division that began the Sunni-Shia split."

The Sunnis prevailed and chose a successor to be the first caliph.

Eventually, Ali was chosen as the fourth caliph, but not before violent conflict broke out. Two of the earliest caliphs were murdered. War erupted when Ali became caliph, and he too was killed in fighting in the year 661 near the town of Kufa, now in present-day Iraq.

The violence and war split the small community of Muslims into two branches that would never reunite.

The Muslim Conquests, which began after Muhammad's death are well documented and large swathes of the Old World—from the India in the east, to Spain in the west—were conquered and consolidated by the sword of Islam during this time, with more after (e.g., the Ottoman conquests). The first major conquest, renowned for its brutality, occurred in Arabia itself, immediately after Muhammad's death in 632. Many tribes which had only nominally accepted Islam's authority, upon Muhammad's death, figured they could break away; however, Muhammad's successor and first caliph, or successor, Abu Bakr, would have none of that, and proclaimed a jihad against these apostates, known in Arabic as the "Ridda Wars" (or Apostasy Wars). According to the aforementioned historians, tens of thousands of Arabs were put to the sword until their tribes re-submitted to Islam.

The Ridda Wars ended around 634. To keep the Arab Muslims from quarreling, the next caliph, Omar, launched the Muslim conquests: Syria was conquered around 636, Egypt 641, Mesopotamia and the Persian Empire, 650. By the early 8th century, all of north Africa and Spain to the west, and the lands of central Asia and India to the east, were also brought under Islamic suzerainty.

638 AD : The Arab conquest began 1300 years of Muslim presence in what then became known as Filastin. (Arab word for Palestine). Eager to be rid of their Byzantine overlords and aware of their shared heritage with the Arabs, the descendants of Ishmael, as well as the Muslims reputation for mercy and compassion in victory, the people of Jerusalem handed over the city after a brief siege. They made only one condition, that the terms of their surrender be negotiated directly with the Khalif 'Umar in person. 'Umar entered Jerusalem on foot. There was no bloodshed. There were no massacres. Those who wanted to leave were allowed to, with all their goods. Those who wanted to stay were guaranteed protection for their lives, their property and places of worship.

Palestine was holy to Muslims because the Prophet Muhammad had designated Jerusalem as the first qibla (the direction Muslims face when praying) and because he was believed to have ascended on a night journey to heaven from the old city of Jerusalem (al-Aqsa Mosque today) where the Dome of the Rock was later built. Jerusalem became the third holiest city of Islam. The Muslim rulers did not force their religion on the Palestinians, and more than a century passed before the majority converted to Islam. The remaining Christians and Jews were considered People of the Book. They were allowed autonomous control in their communities and guaranteed security and freedom of worship. Such tolerance was rare in the history of religion. Most Palestinians also adopted Arabic and Islamic culture. Palestine benefited from the empire's trade and from its religious significance during the first Muslim dynasty, the Umayyads of Damascus.

750 AD: The power shifted to Baghdad with the Abbasids, Palestine became neglected. It suffered unrest and successive domination by Seljuks, Fatimids, and European Crusaders. It shared, however, in the

glory of Muslim civilization, when the Muslim world enjoyed a golden age of science, art, philosophy, and literature. Muslims preserved Greek learning and broke new ground in several fields, all of which later contributed to the Renaissance in Europe. Like the rest of the empire, however, Palestine under the Mamelukes gradually stagnated and declined. Five centuries of peaceful coexistence elapsed before political events led to centuries of so-called holy wars

But elsewhere over the next fourteen centuries, the bloody legacy of this extraordinary individual Muhammad, would be a constant challenge to those living on the borders of the Islam's political power. The violence that Muslim armies would visit on people across North Africa, the Middle East, Europe and into Asia as far as the Indian subcontinent is a tribute to a founder who practiced and promoted subjugation, rape, murder and forced conversion.

In Muhammad's words: "I have been ordered to fight the people till they say: 'None has the right to be worshipped but Allah.' And if they say so, pray like our prayers, face our Qibla and slaughter as we slaughter, then their blood and property will be sacred to us and we will not interfere with them..." (Bukhari 8:387)

It is certainly the basis not just for modern day terror campaigns against Western infidels (and Hindus and Buddhists) but also the broad apathy that Muslims across the world have to the violence, which is an obvious enabler.

As Indonesian cleric, Abu Bakar Bashir recently put it, "If the West wants to have peace, then they have to accept Islamic rule."

Maybe a separation should have been made – Islam as true 'religion' of God and Muhammadism for followers of this madman in their quest for subjugation and power.

Worth inserting here is a speech given by Winston Churchill in 1899 when he was a young soldier and journalist:

"How dreadful are the curses which Mohammedanism lays on its votaries! Besides the fanatical frenzy, which is as dangerous in a man as hydrophobia in a dog, there is this fearful fatalistic apathy. The effects are apparent in many countries, improvident habits, slovenly systems of agriculture, sluggish methods of commerce, and insecurity of property exist wherever the followers of the Prophet rule or live.

A degraded sensualism deprives this life of its grace and refinement, the next of its dignity and sanctity. The fact that in Mohammedan law every woman must belong to some man as his absolute property, either as a child, a wife, or a concubine, must delay the final extinction of slavery until the faith of Islam has ceased to be a great power among men.

Individual Muslims may show splendid qualities, but the influence of the religion paralyses the social development of those who follow it.

No stronger retrograde force exists in the world. Far from being moribund, Mohammedanism is a militant and proselytizing faith. It has already spread throughout Central Africa, raising fearless warriors at every step; and were it not that Christianity is sheltered in the strong arms of science, the science against which it had vainly struggled, the civilization of modern Europe might fall, as fell the civilization of ancient Rome."

12

CRUSADER DOMINATION AND THE GREAT SCHISM
1000 AD to 1300 AD

'Halliday, Fred, 100 myths about the Middle East'

"The city of Jerusalem has for centuries been an object of reverence and longing on the part of Christians, Jews and Muslims. Contemporary Jerusalem 'is' or alternatively 'should be', by some divine ordinance wholly Jewish, or Muslim, or Arab, or something.

Christians have made much of Jerusalem as the site of the crucifixion of Jesus Christ, but other centers of political and religious power - notably Rome and Byzantium (but also, for Orthodox Christians, Kiev and, for Armenians, St Echmiatsin) - have historically been more important. The sacking of Jerusalem by the Crusaders in 1099 and the massacre of its Muslim and Jewish inhabitants showed little respect for that city, and it was a dispute over the keys to the Church of the Holy Sepulchre which sparked the Crimean War in 1854.

After 638 AD Jerusalem (and Palestine) were under Muslim rule and because these places were considered holy the inhabitants were allowed to keep their places of worship and their properties and were even allowed to leave if they so wished. The majority converted to Islam of their own free will and the remaining Christians and Jews were considered "People of the Book". So even at the time of the First

Crusade, 1095 AD, and the capture of Jerusalem in 1099 AD, Palestine and in particular Jerusalem were enjoying some religious freedom even if the rest of the world wasn't. There was infighting between the different Islamic factions and at the time of the First Crusade, Palestine was controlled by the Fatimids who also maintained their lenient religious approach even though at that time the area was reeling under some neglect. It seems that maybe the reason for the First Crusade was not so much to rescue Jerusalem from Islam but possibly the western world and in particular the Papacy objected to the fact that the whole of the Middle East was under the Islamic rule, thereby making it a political decision to try to change that."

The extent of the Islamic rule at the time of the First Crusade, lands not won by peaceable means by any stretch of the imagination was vast and further expansion of Islam is obviously encroaching on areas that the western world deemed "not for sale". East and West is rapidly becoming more defined.

Many of us are surprised to learn that for the first 1000 years of Christian history there was just one Church. It was in the eleventh century that a disastrous split occurred between Orthodox East and Latin West. Although it had been brewing for years, the so-called "Great Schism" of 1054 represented a formal—and shocking— separation between Rome and Orthodoxy. At the core of the controversy were two vitally important areas of disagreement: the role of the papacy, and the manner in which doctrine is to be interpreted.

The spirit of Christianity which was nurtured in the East had a particular flavour. It was distinct, though not necessarily opposed, to that which developed in the Western portion of the Roman Empire and subsequent Medieval Kingdoms in the West. While Christianity in the West developed in lands which knew the legal and moral philosophy of Ancient Rome, Eastern Christianity developed in lands which knew the Semitic and Hellenistic cultures. While the West was concerned with the Passion of Christ and the sin of man, the East emphasized the Resurrection of Christ and the deification of man. While the West leaned toward a legalistic view of religion, the East espoused a more mystical theology. Since the Early Church was not monolithic, the two great traditions existed together for more than a thousand years until the Great Schism divided the Church. Today, Roman Catholics and Protestants are heirs to the Western tradition, and the Orthodox are heirs to the Eastern tradition.

Christians of the Eastern Churches call themselves Orthodox. This description comes to us from the fifth century and has two meanings which are closely related. The first definition is "true teaching." The Orthodox Church believes that she has maintained and handed down the Christian faith, free from error and distortion, from the days of the Apostles. The second definition, which is actually the more preferred, is "true praise." To bless, praise, and glorify God the Father, Son, and Holy Spirit is the fundamental purpose of the Church. All her activities, even her doctrinal formulations, are directed toward this goal.

Occasionally, the word Catholic is also used to describe the Orthodox Church. This description, dating back to the second century, is embodied in the Nicene Creed, which acknowledges One, Holy, Catholic, and Apostolic Church. From the Orthodox perspective, Catholic means that the Church is universal and also that she includes persons of all races and cultures. It also affirms that the Church has preserved the fullness of the Christian faith. It is not unusual for titles such as Greek, Russian, and Antiochian to be used in describing Orthodox Churches. These appellations refer to the cultural or national roots of a particular parish, diocese, or archdiocese.

One of the threads of this book is the divisions that have occurred in "religion", the other thread being the associated violence. So the "Great Schism" earns an extended mention, because the reasons for it are purely of a human nature. Non acceptance of the status quo, control required over all Christian peoples, demand of compliance with priestly interpretations of existing scriptures, rules, regulations and obedience to one person – The Pope – and as shall be seen in later chapters this demand of compliance will be enforced in a terrible and non-Christian way. It seems that after one thousand years the gulf between what God wanted and what God is getting is wider than ever and the gulf will continue to widen. The Catholic Church appears to have forgotten what faith or belief in God actually means, drifting more towards politics and power – AGAIN!

So much for the "Great Schism" and now to return to the 'Crusades". I was always led to believe that 'The Crusades" was a great Christian event that saved the Western world from becoming a Godless waste but after some review and being made aware of the violence and butchery that was part and parcel of the Christian Crusader (knights, mostly), the facts appear to show absolutely no difference between the manner of fighting between the 'good guys' and the 'bad guys'. Maybe that was the only way, but the Pope and his henchmen did not hesitate to use whatever means they had at their disposal to settle two problems, and the following passage describe those events:

It is usually assumed that the reason for the Crusades was primarily the Islamic expansion and the Muslim control of territories in The Holy Land and surrounding areas but a second, more pressing problem for the Pope was the rivalry between Roman and Byzantine cultures. The Byzantine model had always been that each bishop was independent and equal. The Roman model was that the bishop of Rome, the Pope, was supreme. An uneasy truce remained in place until 1064 when the Eastern churches flatly refused to submit to the pope. This split, as mentioned, is called the Great Schism.

A reform movement called the Cluniac was trying to restore discipline to the church around this time and with the naming of Urban 11 to the papacy in 1088, this event led to attempts to reassert control over the Eastern Church but events in the Muslim world, specifically when the Turks invaded Persia, focused attention in another direction. Anatolia, which was the center of the Byzantine Empire, was lost to the Turks and this loss heralded the end of the Byzantine Empire. The Turkish invasion also disrupted pilgrim traffic to and from the Holy Land and supposedly this disruption was the primary reason for the Crusades but maybe not......

Pope Urban 11 called for the Crusade in 1095, primarily to drive the Turks out of Anatolia but his hidden agenda was to heal the Great Schism on Rome's terms by rescuing the Byzantines and obligating them. The objective of going on to reconquer the Holy Land, which no doubt had everyone's approval, was not the Pope's biggest concern but 'who knew'?

The question has been asked, why, if the Pope could commandeer a force of 60,000 men to head east, why had he not done so before. The possible answer is that the first Crusade was an Eastern project devised and inspired not by Pope Urban 11 but by Alexios 1 of the Byzantine Empire. Alexios, under tremendous pressure from Turkish warlords, issued pleas for help across Western Europe including one to Pope Urban 11, which brought with it the offer to unite the Catholic and Orthodox churches once and for all. What followed was less a war to protect the Holy Land than a defence of the Byzantine Empire. So rather than being under the command of the Pope, the knights were controlled by Alexios but knights being knights they refused to give up what they had conquered and eventually Alexios lost control. As a result history was kind of re-written with Alexios and Byzantine removed from font row and center and Pope Urban 11 moved to center stage. In short, the knights heroic and glorious deeds, recorded in such lavish style by historians and celebrated ever since was merely a cover story. Maybe this only applies to the First Crusade?

To continue with the First Crusade saga, eventually the Crusaders were organized and embarked from Constantinople around 1096-97. They retook the ancient city of Nicaea but were prevented from looting it by the Byzantine emperor's troops much to their dismay. So it appears pretty obvious that the main intent of this first lot of Crusaders was to plunder and fill their pockets, all in the name of Christendom of course. Forgetting the morals and lack of scruples of these paid thugs in armour, they did achieve some success in the Holy Land. They did not defeat the Turks but did enough to halt their expansion and provide a basis for future Crusades. They marched into Palestine, captured Jerusalem and indulged in wholesale massacre and plundering. How on earth did the Crusades ever deserve a name commiserate with the forces of Good overcoming the forces of Evil? The strange outcome of this particular act was the lack of response from the Muslim powers. It is possible that Palestine was not of sufficient strategic importance being sandwiched between Egypt and Persia even though Jerusalem was just as much a Holy City for the Muslims as it was for Christians and Jews but Palestine still should have been held by the Crusaders and could have been held if a little bit of military tactical thought had been employed but it was not be. In fact the opposite happened, instead of trying to re-establish friendly relations with their neighbours they believed that they could eventually overcome Islam itself. They actually enlisted the help of at least one Muslim ruler to do this and predictably the Crusader citadel of Edessa was lost because of this mistaken confidence in receiving help from the opposition.

A Second Crusade was launched in 1147 but military leadership was so inept that even with the help of moderate Muslims (there were still areas where Muslims and Christians lived side by side in relative peaceful harmony contrary to beliefs that this was not the case), the Second Crusade was a disaster and once Saladin took over leadership of the Muslims and demonstrated his military skills, all faith and confidence that any Muslims still had in the Crusaders vanished and eventually Saladin invaded Palestine in 1187 and re-took Jerusalem.

The consequent Third Crusade (1189-92), whilst the Crusader forces had made some gains and treaty rights had been secured for pilgrims to visit Jerusalem, the relations between the Western forces and Byzantine had become extremely strained. Nevertheless a Fourth Crusade was planned.

The following dozen or so paragraphs are mostly taken from the Internet's University of Phoenix syllabus – The Crusades and Medieval Christianity Section 15 by Prof. Mark Damen:

"If crusading was to continue at all, it was going to need some serious restructuring. Having failed in so many respects, the Third Crusade entailed disappointments no one in Europe could ignore. For one, it hadn't returned Jerusalem and the Holy Lands to Christian control. For another, it had led to bitter in-fighting within Europe—which ran directly counter to its Truce-of-God mission to repress wars on the home front and that was, at least in part, because it hadn't deflected the restless aggression of Europe's knights outside the West—by these standards, the Third Crusade might as well not have happened at all, which helps to explain why the **Fourth Crusade** followed so swiftly on its heels.

Meanwhile, there were other changes afoot within the European community. In particular, by the beginning of the thirteenth century, the papacy had found a strong advocate in **Innocent III**, the most effective pope in Medieval history. This young, intelligent pontiff had been trained in law and thus spoke the language of international diplomacy better than most political rulers in Europe, indeed as well as the best statesmen ever have. His ability to craft strategies promoting the interests of the Church and to put them into effect is unparalleled in Western history, so he gave the next crusade a professional appearance of a sort the Crusades had never enjoyed before. Nevertheless, Europe would soon learn that amateurism suited crusading better." Pope Innocent 111 is usually considered the founder of the Papal state and history has it that he organized the Fourth Crusade to recapture Jerusalem.

"Yet with Innocent spearheading the venture, it was bound to succeed somehow. The pontiff began by doing his history homework and devised a means by which to avoid the hazards which had scuttled the last two Crusades. What had drowned the most recent one was the division of leadership among three kings, and Innocent resolved to avoid that error by putting himself in charge alone. What had foundered the Second Crusade was the treachery of the double-dealing Byzantines, so the decision was made to send the next wave of crusaders by sea, enabling them to avoid Byzantium completely—that the Fourth Crusade would eventually end up in downtown Constantinople is a rousing tribute to human folly, not an indictment of Innocent's plan—and if everything had gone the way he arranged it, it would have been a perfectly fine Crusade. But the best-laid plans of popes and men . . .

There are more ways than one, however, for a large contingent of warriors to earn their passage across the sea. For instance, **Zara**, one of Venice's subject states on the eastern shore of the Adriatic Sea, had recently revolted from the city's burgeoning maritime empire and, to avoid Venetian reprisal, the people of Zara had delivered their city into the Pope's warm and all-welcoming embrace. Zara was now one of the Papal States, a burgeoning empire of its own currently under construction by the Roman Church.

In exchange for cash-on-delivery, the Venetians contracted with the crusaders to stop in at Zara on their way out east and force it back under Venice's thumb. Such an agreement was certainly *not* part of Innocent's plan for this Crusade—that is, his goals did not include that the crusaders he'd assembled would strip his papacy of newly-won territory—and when he learned about their agreement with the Venetians, he withdrew his support of the Crusade, along with his funding. And when that didn't stop them, he laid a writ of **excommunication** on them all— that is, he effectively ousted them from the Church, condemning their souls to perdition—but that, too, made exactly zero difference in their arrangements. The crusaders sailed to Zara and duly delivered it back into Venetian hands.

While lingering in the area, the crusaders came across a Byzantine exile, a pretender to the throne who had recently been exiled from Byzantium and who offered them a substantial sum if they would put him on the throne. With the sanction of the Venetians who saw nothing but advantage in causing turmoil within Byzantium, their trading rival in the Mediterranean, the crusaders were diverted again from the Holy Lands. This time they headed in the direction of Constantinople.

There, the crusaders' approach inspired considerable panic among the Byzantines, not an unreasonable reaction as this now well-funded, sea-borne assault force bore down on them. The reigning Emperor, along with many others, fled Constantinople. Thus, meeting no real resistance, the crusaders entered the city and set their "Latin" nominee for Emperor on the throne, then turned around and headed for the Holy Lands at last—so far, this expedition could hardly be called a crusade, more a floating band of hitmen-for-hire—but now these Zara-siegers and Byzantine-kingmakers were at last on their way to becoming true crusaders, for the moment anyway.

However, almost as soon as they sailed out of Constantinople's harbor, their "Latin" pretender was murdered. When the news of his assassination reached them, the crusaders turned their ships around and headed back to secure the situation, if for nothing else, to fortify their supply lines. Their earlier treacheries would now come back to haunt the Byzantines. When the crusaders found the city bolted tight against them, the stage was set for a siege and the odds were strongly in the Byzantines' favour. In all the centuries since its founding by the Roman Emperor Constantine in the early fourth century, Constantinople had never succumbed to an assault from outside.

But contrary to historical precedent, these crusading marauders who seemed determined to fight anyone **but** Moslems accomplished the seemingly impossible. At long last the heavens failed Byzantium and its capital city fell to siege for the first time ever, and not at the hands of Moslems or Vikings or Mongols—not that all of those hadn't at some point tried to take Constantinople—but to the descendants of the Byzantines' closest relatives, western Europeans, the **other** heirs of Rome. To put it another way, when Constantine's "New Rome" finally fell, it fell to the original Rome.

The resulting **Sack of Constantinople** in 1204 lasted three days, though its tremors are still felt today. For one, the great library there was destroyed when the crusaders ransacked it, even stabling their horses there—it's unimaginable how much ancient learning and literature was lost in that catastrophe—it's almost certain the complete works of some ancient authors whose writings now exist only in tattered fragments, some entirely lost, were housed in this library once. Worse yet, the fire set in that dark year became a cataclysmic blaze two centuries later.

In 1453, the Turks relit the flames of siege and took the city once and for all, exterminating Byzantium at long last. Thus, ironically, it was the Christian crusaders' siege of Constantinople that paved the way for the Moslems' eventual takeover of the entire area. Constantinople is now Istanbul, an Islamic site.

In besieging two cities—and neither of which was Moslem at the time—the men of the Fourth Crusade clearly thought they had done enough. Feeling no particular need to proceed on to the Holy Lands, they returned to Europe with their spoils of conquest, and given that they had briefly re-united East and West, healing momentarily the schism in the Church, Innocent III had little choice but to forgive and "re-communicate" the crusaders. So, they paraded in triumph, bearing the plunder of the East: gold, relics and all sorts of memorabilia, though nary a book of learning. In fact, remarkably little of any intellectual substance would come of the ransacked Byzantines. It was as if all Europe in the aftermath of the Fourth Crusade was collectively wearing a souvenir shirt that read, "My uncle sacked Constantinople, and all I got was some bronze horses."

Remember the original aim of healing the Great Schism? It was now forever out of reach. The Byzantines preferred surrender to the Turks in 1453 to seeking aid from the West. Not until the 1960's did a Pope and Greek Orthodox patriarch meet in person.

Innocent 111 is also remembered as the Pope who authorized the Dominican Order – founded by St. Dominic of Spain – to convert Muslims and Jews and put an end to heresy in 1216. This Dominican order eventually became the main administrator of Inquisition trials.

Meanwhile, Jerusalem was still in the hands of the Moslems. The Fifth Crusade attempted a quite different strategy. The Crusaders would capture the port of Damietta at the mouth of the Nile, bottle up Egypt's commerce, and swap the port for Jerusalem. Damietta was besieged in 1218-1219 and the sultan of Egypt finally agreed to the swap. By this time, the Crusaders, suffering from megalomania, decided to attempt the conquest of all of Egypt. They were stranded by the annual Nile flood and had to retreat, miraculously snatching defeat from the jaws of victory.

Frederick II of Germany had promised to lead a Crusade in 1215, finally started on the Sixth Crusade in 1227, and turned back. For this he was excommunicated. He finally landed in Palestine and in 1229, after little fighting and much negotiation, concluded a treaty that gave the Crusaders Jerusalem and all the other holy cities and a truce of ten years - more than they had achieved by all the previous failed Crusades. He was widely condemned for conducting the Crusade by negotiating rather than fighting.

With that sort of thinking, it is no surprise that the peace did not last long and that the Crusaders again lost Jerusalem in 1244. King Louis IX of France, the patron saint of France and the Saint Louis after whom the city and Louisiana are named, led the Crusade. Louis was brave in battle, kind to his friends, generous to his enemies, pious, a truly noble man, and hopelessly incompetent as a general. The events of the Seventh Crusade (1248-1254) are almost exactly a replay of the Fifth: attack Damietta, agree to trade it for Jerusalem, succumb to an attack of hubris, attempt to conquer Egypt, lose it all. A militant dynasty, the Mamelukes, came to power in Egypt and soon swept most of the Crusader strongholds remaining in Palestine. In 1252 The Papacy approves the use of torture for religious disobedience following Innocent 111's brutal Inquisition.

(The Mamelukes arose from an institution that has been used at times in the East but has no counterpart in the West - a slave army. The reasoning seems to be that soldiers are bound to obedience anyway, so they might as well be slaves. Don't get the image of whips and poverty - they may have been slaves in the legal sense but were better off than most other members of their societies. Invariably, sooner or later, the slaves eventually reasoned "We're the ones with the swords. Why should we be slaves?" and staged a coup, as the Mamelukes did in Egypt.)

The Eighth and last Crusade (1270) is in some ways the most poignant. One can easily picture Louis, now in middle age, a bit bored, the chain mail a bit snug at the waist perhaps, reminiscing about his youth as a Crusader, and deciding to have one more try at it. His brother, Charles of Anjou, king of Sicily, had strategic plans of his own in the eastern Mediterranean and did not want a Crusade interfering with them. He diverted the expedition to Tunisia, where Louis died. The last Crusader cities on the mainland of Palestine fell in 1291; one small island stronghold lasted until 1303.

With Louis' death, the Crusades died out with a whimper and not a bang. Continued military failure was a principal reason for their end. For a chronicle of military and political ineptitude, coupled with sheer hubris, they have no comparison in history. The Crusaders had victory in their grasp **four times**. They won the First Crusade in battle, had a trade almost in hand in the Fifth and Seventh Crusades, and negotiated a victory in the Sixth Crusade, and in the end they still managed to lose it all. Where else can we find a war that was won **four times** and still finally lost? Even the most ardent backers of Crusades were able to see eventually that the strategy was not working. Moreover, Europe in 1270 was a very different place than it was in 1087. Rising European prosperity and the increasing interest in internal affairs helped to lessen interest in the Crusades. The concept of crusading was also discredited by "crusades" against Christians (for example, aberrant sects like the Albigensians) or rulers who otherwise displeased the Pope.

Perhaps the most significant effect of the Crusades was a vast increase in cultural horizons for many Europeans. For every European who went on a Crusade (let alone the minuscule fraction who returned) there were hundreds who knew someone who had gone, or who had seen the Crusaders march by. Palestine was no longer a quasi-mythical place that people knew only from Bible readings in church; it was a real place where real people went. Once Crusader kingdoms, however fragile, were set up in Palestine, they traded with their kin in Europe, sending finished goods to Europe and importing raw materials. The result was a stimulus to Mediterranean trade. The need to transfer large sums of money for troops and supplies led to development of banking and accounting techniques. If the combatants in the Crusades came mostly from France, Germany and England, the middlemen tended to be merchants from northern Italy. The Crusades launched the economic dominance of cities like Genoa and Venice. The financial burdens of the Crusades, coupled with the need to borrow money to finance them, weakened the power of the nobility and strengthened the merchant classes and the independence of cities.

The cultural and technological enrichment was primarily from East to West; Europe was underdeveloped by Middle Eastern standards and had little to give in return. The principal effects of the Crusades on the Moslem world were negative. Europe lost prestige and military status in the eyes of Moslems, perhaps encouraging the later Turkish incursions into the Balkans. The Moslem world was already becoming more intellectually and theologically conservative; the Crusades accelerated the process and further undermined the long tradition of tolerance in the Moslem world. However, while the Crusaders were making minor nuisances of themselves pecking away at the Moslem world from the West, the Moslem world was about to receive a sledgehammer blow from the East: the Mongol invasions.

All wars are terrible – no matter in what epoch they are fought. Or with what weapons, but the wars of the Catholic Church against the heresy of Catharism in the thirteenth century, the so called Albigensian Crusades, must rank high on the list of the most repulsive, brutal and merciless conflicts that human beings have ever had the misfortune to be involved in. The Cathars are innocent in these matters by any sane standards of justice. All they did was reject the authority of the Pope and give their loyalty to another religion. And hasn't that just been the case over the years?

No one can dispute that the Roman Catholic Church has a long track record of vigorous opposition to all forms of knowledge, scripture, inquiry, wisdom and religious self-expression that do not accord with its own views. It was mobs of Christians, aroused by Theophilis the Catholic Archbishop of Alexandria, who sacked the Serapeum in Alexandria in 391 AD. They killed all the pagans and Gnostics who had taken shelter inside it and razed to the ground the wonderful library that had been arranged around its cloisters together with its entire irreplaceable collection of ancient books and scrolls. This is just one of many atrocities in the ruthless suppression of Gnosticism and paganism by the Catholic Church and its generally very efficient destruction of their texts and traditions. Who knew?

Without getting into any issues regarding the above sects, they all regarded themselves as Christians. Obviously interpretation of the scriptures accounts for their views, but the Gnostics, Bogomils and Cathars had much in common. Unfortunately for them, they were all classed as heretics and persecuted by the church, which, in the early centuries AD was the Roman Catholic Church. The Roman Catholic Church's dogma was the enforcement of blind obedience and violent intolerance for the beliefs of others and was their stock in trade right from the beginning. In fact, such was the relentless harassment of the 'non-believers' that around the fifth century that the First Inquisition was born. Historians have little doubt that proto-Catholics deliberately manipulated the gradual formation of the New Testament so that it could serve them in their early battles against the Gnostics and reinforce their own claims to authenticity and exclusivity as the sole mediators of Christ's message.

Though its defenders claim otherwise, there is no superior logic in whatsoever in the Catholic position and yet the Catholic Church grows stronger whilst the Orthodox Church remains basically Eastern and the Jews remain well…… er Jewish, and "religion" remains as confusing and violently focused as ever.

13
RELIGION AND EUROPE
1300 AD to 1500 AD

In the 1300s Europeans faced the constant threat of famine—mass starvation. Harvests had been poor and mass hunger a serious danger in 1305-1314; then, in 1315-1322, famine devastated most of Europe. Spring and Summer floods led to crop failures, so that peasants had absolutely no surplus grain to sell at market in fall 1315; things were so bad in winter 1315-1316 that peasants ate the seed that they had stored for the Spring planting. Therefore they had little to plant in Spring 1316, which together with bad weather made that another famine year. It took more than five years to break this cycle. Making matters worse was a wave of "epizootics" (epidemic diseases among animals) that destroyed much of Europe's livestock. This not only added to the problems of agriculture by killing off draft animals, but also deprived people of meat and dairy products.

The results of starvation were devastating. Tens of thousands of people simply starved to death. Epidemic illnesses carried off tens of thousands more whose resistance to disease had been weakened by hunger. At least one in every ten people in Europe perished in the famines and epidemics of 1315-1316. Still, the population exceeded Europe's agricultural capacity. With demand high and grain supplies low, prices for food soared. Although the wealthy aristocracy continued to live in luxury and seldom went without, hunger remained a constant for the mass of the rural and urban poor.

In 1347, though, a new plague struck Europe and hit rich and poor alike: the Black Death. Although there is some debate among historians as to the epidemiology of the Black Death, most historians argue that this was the Plague (in two forms, bubonic and pneumonic). According to the dominant theory, the Plague had begun in Mongolia then in the early 1300s was carried by rats and fleas to lands that the Mongol armies had conquered in the previous century--China, Northern India, and Russ. Italian ships trading with the Russ cities on the Black Sea had accidentally transported disease-carrying rats and fleas back to Genoa. The disease then spread along trade routes through Italy and into Western and Central Europe. Those bitten by infected fleas died horrible deaths within a week's time; those who inhaled the virus died much more quickly but no less horridly. Within a generation, Plagued had killed off 40 percent of the English population and nearly 60 percent of the population in Northeastern France. The only escape from Plague seemed to be to flee infected districts completely. The mass of death and the flight of populations further undermined agriculture and added to the constant threat of famine.

The Hundred Years' War

The governments of France and England added to these natural calamities by carrying out a series of long, deadly wars, which are known collectively as the Hundred Years' War (1337-1453), and which aggravated the problem of agricultural decline. The Hundred Years' War had its roots in three situations: the English kings' continuing claim to territories in France and the efforts of the French crown to push them out; English support for the Flemish rebellion against French rule; and a succession crisis when both English King Edward III and the new French King Philip Valois (Philip IV) both claimed to be the rightful successor to the French Capetian King Charles IV died without an heir. The war took place entirely in France, and contributed to the loss of lives and farmland.

One common response to the multiple disasters and hardships of the 1300s was to conclude that God was passing judgment on mankind's sins. This was not a surprising response given the new trends in popular Christian practice. Tens of thousands of devout concluded that the

Church had failed to satisfy their spiritual needs, often because they saw the clergy as too worldly. One very common means of filling this spiritual hunger was to engage in pilgrimages to holy sites (which became much more common in the 1300s). Another was to follow the example of early Christian hermits, who thought that punishing the flesh was a means of feeding the spirit: these were the flagellants, who joined self-mutilating and self-beating sects (which also proliferated in the 1300s).

While some Europeans sought to beat sin out of themselves, others became absorbed in mysticism, which led (in the Church's view) to heresy. Following the writings of the Dominican priest Master Eckart (1260-1327), for instance, many faithful believed they could commune with God by turning their back on the worldly and meditating on "the spiritual mysteries of Christ." The Church recognized that such views implied that man did not need the Church or the priesthood to achieve salvation, and eventually condemned the circle of Eckart's disciples for the "Heresy of the Free Spirit." Many of the literate men and women who had access to numerous popular tracts such as Thomas Kempis' **Imitation of Christ** (written in the 1420s), also believed that they could achieve salvation by emulating the life of Jesus and contemplating the Bible's mysteries, if they also took what they considered the most important sacrament of the Church—the Eucharist. From the perspective of the Church, the problem with this (again) was that it also undermined the theological significance of the Church and priesthood.

One of the most doctrinally complex forms of heresy to emerge in the 1300s were the teachings of English theologian John Wyclif (1330-1384), who (like St. Augustine) argued that God had predestined only some souls for salvation and the rest for damnation. All Christians could do, Wyclif concluded, was live simply and obey the teachings of Christ. From this, Wyclif reasoned that the Church's sacraments were unnecessary and that so was the Church administration. The Church, he concluded, did little more that provide worldly power and wealth to priests and Bishops, whom he condemned as sinners. Wyclif died before he could be convicted of heresy; after his death, though, thousands of his followers (called Lollards) took up his teachings and rejected the Church. In response to the growth of the Lollard movement, the

Church in England declared this heresy punishable by death (in 1401). Persecution of the Lollards led them to rebel in 1414, but they were easily crushed. Lollardism faded in popularity after 1414, but it did not go away.

In 1303, Pope Boniface VII died soon after having been captured by the army of French King Philip IV, who in the culmination of a long dispute between the two over the King's power over the French clergy had accused the pope of heresy. Philip then forced the new Pope Clement V not only to defend the King's actions, but to live under French guard in Avignon, a "papal city" in southern France. In Church History this situation, which lasted until 1378, is called the Babylonian Captivity (the term comes from the captivity of the Hebrews in Babylon because the Pope became in effect subservient to the French King. There were advantages for the Papacy: it was now isolated from political turmoil in Italy; moreover, French protection allowed the Papacy to consolidate its administrative bureaucracy and its financial system (in addition, the French crown now provided the Papacy with large payments in return for the right to appoint bishops). But the popular perception of the Papacy and the bishops as vassals of France, and the perception that ecclesiastical officers lived in luxury while missions of Christians were starving and suffering, combined to damage the legitimacy of the Church. (This is clear if we consider the heretical movements discussed above.)

In 1388, after the death of Pope Gregory XI, the College of Cardinals named an Italian bishop (Urban VI) as the new pope. But only months later, the Cardinals reversed their decision and appointed a French bishop (Clement VII) as the new pope. Urban VI, who refused to step down, responded by naming a new College of Cardinals and declared that he would rule the Church from Rome, Clement VII insisted that he was the rightful pope, and that he would rule the Church from Avignon. So began another "Great Schism," in which the bishops of Europe declared loyalty to one pope or the other, and the two camps denounced each other as heretics. The split outlived both Urban and Clement, and the rival French and Italian papacies continued battling. (Things became even more confusing when a gathering of bishops in Pisa appointed a third rival pope in 1409). The dispute was not settled until the Council of Constance in 1417. The impact of all this infighting was to further discredit the Church in the eyes of tens of thousands of the faithful, which again helps us understand polar heresies of the 1300s.

Although in the early 1400s the European economy had begun to recover, in other aspects of European life instability continued for several more decades. One example of ongoing religious unrest was the spread of a popular heretical movement in Bohemia.

In Bohemia (the Czech lands of the Holy Roman Empire), some of the English theologian John Wyclif's ideas took root in the teachings of the charismatic preacher Jan Hus (1373-1415). Already by 1400, Hus had translated the Christian Bible into Czech and encouraged laypeople to study it for themselves, rather than rely on the clergy. Around 1408, Hus began echoing Wyclif's views on the worldly corruption of the Church. Central to Hus' theology was Ultraquism—the belief that in the Eucharist the laity should take both the bread (consecrated as Christ's body) and the wine (consecrated as Christ's blood). [In the medieval church, only the priests drank the communion wine]. Huss attracted tens of thousands of supporters among the poor, to whom his call for reform offered hope.

The Hussite movement had political as well as theological dimensions. The movement received support from the Bohemian aristocracy, which hoped that Church reform would give them possession of Church-owned properties, allow them a greater share of tax and toll revenues, etc.. The Bohemian King also offered Hus support, hoping to take advantage of the Great Schism to win greater independence from the Papacy. In 1415, the Papacy invited Hus to speak at the Council of Constance [a major gathering of prelates, called to discuss the Great Schism], ostensibly to explain his reform ideas. But instead of hearing him out, the Church hierarchy arrested Hus, tried and convicted him of heresy, and burned him at the stake. When news of Hus' death reached his peasant followers in Bohemia, they rose up in rebellion against the Roman Church hierarchy. Again, they had support from aristocrats, who took advantage of the rebellion to seize Church lands. The rebellion on Bohemia challenged not the authority not only of the Papacy, but also of the Holy Roman Emperor. Therefore, the Emperor sent armies of German knights to crush the Hussites in 1420-1421.

An army of militant Hussites known as the Taborites, however, destroyed the Emperor's crusader knights. The Taborites argued that the murder of Hus was the work of the Anti-Christ, signaling the biblical apocalypse. They saw themselves as the servants of God battling the forces of the Devil--the Church hierarchy and the Emperor. (During the horrific events of the 1300s, rumors of the Apocalypse had become quite common across Europe.) Despite their military victories, the Taborites remained a minority in the Hussite movement. By the 1430s, aristocrats had taken over leadership of the Hussite reform movement and steered it in a more conservative, conciliatory direction. In 1434, the Church and the Hussites reached a concord: the Hussites would recognize the authority of the Church, and the Church would allow laypeople in Bohemia to drink the consecrated wine during the Eucharist.

The Council of Constance, at which Hus had been arrested, had been called to find a solution to the Great Schism. In 1417, after two years of debate and discussion, the Council appointed a new pope (Martin V), whom the entire Church hierarchy and Europe's Kings agreed to recognize. This finally brought an end to the Great Schism. But it did not end controversy within the Church hierarchy. The Council also resolved that in matters of Church governance, it itself was superior to the Pope.

This began the so-called "Conciliarist Controversy"—the debate over whether the Pope or the council of prelates exercised sovereignty over the Church (in other words, was the Pope an "absolute monarch" or an executive appointed by the council of prelates). Between 1417 and 1449, the Papacy and the Church Councils wrestled each other for dominance over the Church. By 1449 the Papacy won this battle by gaining support from Europe's temporal rulers. The papacy had agreed to concordats with the Kings of France, England, etc., under which the kings and princes would again appoint bishops and other high ecclesiastical officials in their "local" [national] churches. The Papacy had consolidated its hold over the Church, and now concentrated its energies on strengthening its own temporal rule in central Italy.

It's hard to believe that the above paragraphs pertain to "religion" and God's work and it is not surprising at all to read that the church was discredited in the eyes of tens of thousands of the faithful, not to mention the numbers of non-faithful who probably were not all that surprised at the goings on anyway. What was needed was an anti-church union but then that would have brought the population down to the rock bottom level of the church and with the church's military might there would have been even more bloodshed. It seems ultimate power can be achieved by threats of torture and death and WAS achieved by demonstrating those actions.

Radical reformers such as John Wycliffe (c. 1320-1384) and John Hus (c. 1369-1415) also helped pave the way for the Reformation and Protestant doctrine. They challenged the idea that the Church as an institution controlled the road to salvation by asserting the existence of a personal relationship between the individual and God and by claiming that the Bible was the ultimate source of authority for Christians, not the Church; hence these reformers advocated translations of the Bible into the vernacular. They further attacked the wealth and privileges of the upper clergy, favoring a return to the simplicity of the early church. The Church responded to these challenges with great vigor, declaring them heresies; John Hus was burned at the stake in 1415 during the Council of Constance and the power of the Inquisition was used against others.

The Church clearly refused to reform itself, yet one more reason for the Reformation which Martin Luther set off with the posting of the Ninety-five Theses on the door of Wittenberg Church just over a century later in 1517.

14

THE REFORMATION
AND THE RENAISSANCE
1500 AD to 1900 AD

Unrest in the church and calls for change had been brewing for some time but demands and protests by individuals apparently had no real impact on the authoritative church body.

Well before Luther there were calls for reform from within the Western Church. It seems that the church authorities, the powers that be at the time were straying away from the scriptures and the gospel teachings and were beginning, or had been for some time, introducing their own thoughts and traditions where they thought needed improvement. Isn't this the same theme as previously mentioned that these men of the cloth are interfering in the scriptural teachings and wording. How can they assume the right to do that? So the Reformation was coming, the common theme: less of the church and more of Christ – the Christ of course of the gospels, not of the theologians and canon lawyers. God rest the souls of Luther, Wycliffe, Waldo, Hus and the like for literally committing suicide in their quest for reform. The church authorities saw this as an attempt to take away their easy pickings. Same old story – money, money. Nothing at all to do with God's work.

The Reformation shattered the unity of Western Christendom. It helped to bring about national churches. It led to the wars of religion. The most destructive of those wars was the Thirty Years War within

Germany, then called the Holy Roman Empire, from 1618 to 1648. The Reformation period is generally dated from 1517 to 1648.

Wars of Religion. The Reformers wanted initially to reform the Holy Roman Catholic Church from what they considered its abuses and superstitions. The Bible and the individual conscience replaced the authority of the Pope and the bishops. The Reformers disagreed not only with the Pope but with each other. Several reform movements developed led by Martin Luther, John Calvin, John Knox, and others. When the Catholic Church sought to restore Christian Unity using the Inquisition and the might of the armies of the Spanish Habsburgs, the reformers protested. They became the Protestants. Four main branches of Protestantism developed during the sixteenth century. They were Lutheranism in Germany and the Scandinavian countries; Calvinism in the Netherlands, parts of Switzerland, Scotland, and England; Anglicanism in England; and Anabaptism. Religious differences led to war. Most of these wars pitted Catholics against Protestants and most of the wars of religion were within countries. They were what we might call civil wars. The French Calvinists, the Huguenots, fought against the French monarchy until Henry of Navarre became Henry IV of France. Henry IV issued the Edict of Toleration which remained in place until revoked by Louis XIV. Calvinists fought against Philip II of Spain until they gained their independence by forming the Seven United Provinces of the Netherlands. In the seventeenth century, Calvinists fought against Anglicans in England. Oliver Cromwell briefly established Calvinist dominance until, after his death, the Stuarts were restored in 1660. But, the bloodiest war took place between Lutherans and Catholics within the Holy Roman Empire. The Thirty Years War killed about half the people in Germany. It lasted from 1618 to 1648.

There are enough books and essays on the Reformation to fill a library so no point in belabouring the point but here is a prime example of violence and its association with "religion".

A little about the Renaissance: it's getting away from the book's themes which are to try and understand why religion has become so diversified and why the undeniable thread of religious violence continues but the

Renaissance and the Reformation, apart from occurring around the same time period, do share some common ground.

The Renaissance started in the city-states in Northern Italy after the Black Death. It can be dated broadly between 1350 AD to 1600 AD. There was an Italian Renaissance and a Northern [European] Renaissance. The writings of William Shakespeare in England belong to the Northern Renaissance. The growing fervor of the Reformation, the hostility between Catholics and Protestants, and the ensuing wars of religion brought the Renaissance to an end, but it's worth looking at this chapter's time period (1500 AD – 1900 AD in more detail.

The Renaissance was a time of great social and cultural change in Europe. It was a period characterised by innovation, imagination and creativity. The Renaissance was also a time during which Europe's classical past was revisited and reinvigorated. Much of the inspiration behind cultural movements of the Renaissance came from people's attempts to emulate (imitate and improve) the legacies of classical European societies, such as Ancient Rome and Greece.

The Renaissance also represented a break away from the conformist society and culture of medieval Europe. A conformist society is one in which people strictly follow established rules and practices. Breaking away from this mould, the Renaissance was a time during which new and inventive ideas began to spread and gain influence. Gradually, this decreased the dominance previously held by the Catholic Church.

Until the Renaissance, most Europeans followed the teachings of Catholicism because they had little exposure to any form of education beyond this. Science was not a well-understood concept and very little of what the Church taught people about life was challenged. Those who spoke out against the Church were accused of heresy and labelled a heretic (someone who holds unorthodox beliefs). Heretics were often subject to extremely severe punishments, such as being tortured or burned at the stake in front of the townspeople.

During the Renaissance, however, things started to change. The 14th through to the 16th centuries in Europe were a period of questioning and discovery. People started to think independently and experiment with new ideas and concepts. As more and more advancements were made in the arts and sciences, the Catholic Church began to lose the overwhelming power and influence it had once held over people's beliefs about the world.

Before more discussion on the Reformation and the more prominent figures associated with the Reformation I am going to insert a borrowed comment here:

"**Apocrypha** are statements or claims that are of dubious authenticity. The word's origin is the medieval Latin adjective apocryphus, "secret, or non-canonical", from the Greek adjective ἀπόκρυφος (apocryphos), "obscure", from verb ἀποκρύπτειν (apocryptein), "to hide away".

It is commonly applied in Christian religious contexts involving certain disagreements about biblical canonicity. The pre-Christian-era Jewish translation (into Greek) of holy scriptures known as the Septuagint included the writings in dispute. However, the Jewish canon was not finalized until at least 100–200 years into the Christian era, at which time considerations of Greek language and beginnings of Christian acceptance of the Septuagint weighed against some of the texts. Some were not accepted by the Jews as part of the Hebrew Bible canon. Over several centuries of consideration, the books of the Septuagint were finally accepted into the Christian Old Testament, by 405 CE in the west, and by the end of the fifth century in the east. The Christian canon thus established was retained for over 1,000 years, even after the 11th-century schism that separated the church into the branches known as the Roman Catholic and Eastern Orthodox churches.

Those canons were not challenged until the Protestant Reformation (16th century), when both the Roman Catholic and Eastern Orthodox Churches reaffirmed them. The reformers rejected the parts of the canon that were not part of the Hebrew Bible and established a revised Protestant canon. Thus, concerning the Old Testament books, what is thought of as the "Protestant canon" is actually the final Hebrew canon. The differences can be found by comparing the contents of the

"Protestant" and Catholic Bibles, and they represent the narrowest Christian application of the term **Apocrypha.**

Among some Protestants, apocryphal began to take on extra or altered connotations, not just of dubious authenticity but of spurious or false content, not just obscure but having hidden or suspect motives. Protestants were (and are) not unanimous in adopting those meanings. Martin Luther said "These Books Are Not Held Equal to the Scriptures, but Are Useful and Good to Read". The Church of England agreed, and that view continues today throughout the Lutheran Church, the worldwide Anglican Communion, and many other denominations. Whichever implied meaning is intended, **Apocrypha** was (and is) used primarily by Protestants, in reference to the books of questioned canonicity. Catholics and Orthodox sometimes avoid using the term in contexts where it might be considered disputatious or be misconstrued as yielding on the point of canonicity. Some Protestants publish Bibles that include the apocryphal books in a separate section (rather like an appendix), so as not to intermingle them with their canonical books.

Explaining the Eastern Orthodox Church's canon is made difficult because of differences of perspective with the Roman Catholic Church in the interpretation of how it was done. Those differences (in matters of jurisdictional authority) were contributing factors in the separation of the Roman Catholics and Orthodox around 1054, but the formation of the canon was largely complete (fully complete in the Catholic view) by the fifth century, six centuries before the separation. In the eastern part of the church, it took much of the fifth century also to come to agreement, but in the end it was accomplished. The canonical books thus established by the undivided church became canon for what was later to become Roman Catholic and Eastern Orthodox alike. The East did already differ from the West in not considering every question of canon yet settled, and it subsequently adopted a few more books into its Old Testament. It also allowed consideration of yet a few more to continue not fully decided, which led in some cases to adoption in one or more jurisdictions, but not all. Thus, there are today a few remaining differences of canon among Orthodox, and all Orthodox accept a few more books than appear in the Catholic canon. Protestants accept none of these additional books as canon either, but see them having roughly the same status as the earlier Apocrypha. As Protestant awareness of the Eastern Orthodox increases in nations like the United States, interest in the full Orthodox canon might also increase enough for them to be published in the Apocrypha of some Protestant Bibles. That is not common yet in 2013, so they are not as widely available in English.

Before the fifth century, the Christian writings that were then under discussion for inclusion in the canon but had not yet been accepted were classified in a group known as the ancient <u>antilegomenae</u>. These were all candidates for the New Testament and included several books which were eventually accepted, such as: <u>The Epistle to the Hebrews</u>, <u>2 Peter</u>, <u>3 John</u> and the <u>Revelation of John</u> (Apocalypse). None of those accepted books can be considered Apocryphal now, since all Christendom accepts them as canonical. Of the uncanonized ones, the Early Church considered some heretical but viewed others quite well. Some Christians, in an extension of the meaning, might also consider the non-heretical books to be "apocryphal" along the manner of Martin Luther: not canon, but useful to read. This category includes books such as the <u>Epistle of Barnabas</u>, the <u>Didache</u>, and <u>The Shepherd of Hermas</u> which are sometimes referred to as the <u>Apostolic Fathers</u>.

Q: Which translation of the Bible does the Roman Catholic Church use?

Catholic Answer

Roman is an epithet first commonly used in England after the protestant revolt to describe the Catholic Church. It is never used by the Catholic Church. The Catholic Bible is composed of the Old Testament and the New Testament. The Old Testament is based on the Septuagint, the Greek translation of the Bible that Our Blessed Lord used. Most of the quotes in the New Testament are taken directly from the Septuagint. The New Testament was decided in the fourth and fifth centuries A.D. The Protestants, when they left the Church in the sixteenth century threw out seven books of the Old Testament that they didn't agree with. They used a "council" of Jewish rabbis in the first century after Christ to base their decision on. Of course the Jews threw out the same seven books as they supported Christianity!

The actual "Catholic Bible" was originally all in Greek, the Old Testament was the Septuagint, translated by the Jews in the fourth century (approximately) B.C., and the New Testament was written in Greek. The official Bible was established in the fourth century A.D. and translated into Latin by Jerome in order that the common people could have access to it. At that time, Latin was the standard language for anyone who could read and write. Later, the Church began translating the Bible into native languages for the people that were no longer literate in Latin. The official Bible remains in Latin, to which all translations should adhere.

The Catholic Church uses the Lectionary which is based on the New Vulgate Bible for use in Mass and other services. Catholics are free to use any translation they want as long as it has an Imprimatur and Nilhi Obstat." from Modern Catholic Dictionary by John A. Hardon, S.J. Doubleday & Co., Inc. Garden City, NY 1980

The Reformation – More about John Wycliffe - John Wycliffe (1320-1384) was a theologian and early proponent of reform in the Roman Catholic Church during the 14th century. He initiated the first translation of the Bible into the English language and is considered the main precursor of the Protestant Reformation. Wycliffe was born at Ipreswell (modern Hipswell), Yorkshire, England, between 1320 and 1330; and he died at Lutterworth (near Leicester) December 31, 1384. The Reformer's entrance upon the stage of ecclesiastical politics is usually related to the question of feudal tribute to which England had been rendered liable by King John, which had remained unpaid for thirty-three years until Pope Urban V in 1365 demanded it. Parliament declared that neither John nor any other had the right to subject England to any foreign power. Should the pope attempt to enforce his claim by arms, he would be met with united resistance. Urban apparently recognized his mistake and dropped his claim. But there was no talk of a patriotic uprising. The tone of the pope was, in fact, not threatening, and he did not wish to draw England into the maelstrom of politics of western and southern Europe. Sharp words were bound to be heard in England, because of the close relations of the papacy with France. It is said that on this occasion Wycliffe served as theological counsel to the government, composed a polemical tract dealing with the tribute, and defended an unnamed monk over against the conduct of the government and parliament. This would place the entrance of Wycliffe into politics about 1365-66. But Wycliffe's more important participation began with the Peace Congress at Bruges. There in 1374 negotiations were carried on between France and England, while at the same time commissioners from England dealt with papal delegates respecting the removal of ecclesiastical annoyances. Wycliffe was among these, under a decree dated July 26, 1374. The choice of a harsh opponent of the Avignon system would have broken up rather than furthered the peace negotiations. It seems he was designated purely as a theologian, and so considered himself, since a noted Scripture scholar was required alongside of those learned in civil and canon law. There was no need for a man of renown, or a pure advocate of state interests. His predecessor in a like case was John Owtred, a monk who formulated the statement that St. Peter had united in his hands spiritual and temporal power--the opposite of what Wycliffe taught. In the days of the mission to Bruges Owtred still belonged in Wycliffe's circle of friends.

Wycliffe was still regarded by the Roman Catholic Church as trustworthy; his opposition to the ruling conduct of the Church may have escaped notice. It was difficult to recognize him as a heretic. The controversies in which men engaged at Oxford were philosophical rather than purely theological or ecclesiastical-political, and the method of discussion was academic and scholastic. The kind of men with whom Wycliffe dealt included the Carmelite monk John Kyningham over theological questions (utrum Christus esset humanitas), or ecclesiastical-political ones (De dominatione civili; De dotatione ecclesiae).Wycliffe regarded it as a sin to incite the pope to excommunicate laymen who had deprived wicked clergy of their temporalities, his dictum being that a man in a state of sin had no claim upon government.

Wycliffe blamed the Benedictine and professor of theology at Oxford, William Wynham of St. Albans (where the anti-Wycliffe trend was considerable) for making public controversies which had previously been confined to the academic arena. Wycliffe himself tells (Sermones, iii. 199) how he concluded that there was a great contrast between what the Church was and what it ought to be, and saw the necessity for reform.

His ideas stress the perniciousness of the temporal rule of the clergy and its incompatibility with the teaching of Christ and the apostles, and make note of the tendencies which were evident in the measures of the "Good Parliament".

Wycliffe wanted to see his ideas actualized--his fundamental belief was that the Church should be poor, as in the days of the apostles. He had not yet broken with the mendicant friars, and from these John of Gaunt chose Wycliffe's defenders. While the Reformer later claimed that it was not his purpose to incite temporal lords to confiscation of the property of the Church, the real tendencies of the propositions remained unconcealed. The result of the same doctrines in Bohemia--that land which was richest in ecclesiastical foundations--was that in a short time the entire church estate was taken over and a revolution brought about in the relations of temporal holdings. It was in keeping with the plans of Gaunt to have a personality like Wycliffe on his side. Especially in London the Reformer's views won support; partisans of the nobility attached themselves to him, and the lower orders gladly heard his sermons. He preached in city churches, and London rang with his praises.

The first to oppose his theses were monks of those orders which held possessions, to whom his theories were dangerous. Oxford and the episcopate were later blamed by the Curia, which charged them with so neglecting their duty that the breaking of the evil fiend into the English sheepfold could be noticed in Rome before it was in England. Wycliffe was summoned before William Courtenay, bishop of London, on Feb. 19, 1377, in order "to explain the wonderful things which had streamed forth from his mouth." The exact charges are not known, as the matter did not get as far as a definite examination. Gaunt, the earl marshal Henry Percy, and a number of other friends accompanied Wycliffe, and four begging friars were his advocates. A crowd gathered at the church, and at the entrance of the party animosities began to show, especially in an angry exchange between the bishop and the Reformer's protectors. Gaunt declared that he would humble the pride of the English clergy and their partisans, hinting at the intent to secularize the possessions of the Church.

Most of the English clergy were irritated by this encounter, and attacks upon Wycliffe began, finding their response in the second and third books of his work dealing with civil government. These books carry a sharp polemic, hardly surprising when it is recalled that his opponents charged Wycliffe with blasphemy and scandal, pride and heresy. He appeared to have openly advised the secularization of English church property, and the dominant parties shared his conviction that the monks could better be controlled if they were relieved from the care of secular affairs..... There are whole books about John Wycliffe and so there should be but this is condensed so that what is evident is that the Church saw him as a threat to its power and well-being; following further .... In order to refute his opponents, he wrote the book in which he showed that Holy Scripture contains all truth and, being from God, is the only authority. He referred to the conditions under which the condemnation of his 18 theses was brought about; and the same may be said of his books dealing with the Church, the office of king, and the power of the pope--all completed within the space of two years (1378-79).

Wycliffe wrote, "The Church is the totality of those who are predestined to blessedness. It includes the Church triumphant in heaven... and the Church militant or men on earth. No one who is eternally lost has part in it. There is one universal Church, and outside of it there is no salvation. Its head is Christ. No pope may say that he is the head, for he cannot say that he is elect or even a member of the Church."

The books and tracts of Wycliffe's last six years include continual attacks upon the papacy and the entire hierarchy of his times. Each year they focus more and more, and at the last pope and Antichrist seem to him practically equivalent concepts. Yet there are passages which are moderate in tone; Lechler identifies three stages in Wycliffe's relations with the papacy. The first step, which carried him to the outbreak of the schism, involves moderate recognition of the papal primacy; the second, which carried him to 1381, is marked by an estrangement from the papacy; and the third shows him in sharp contest. However, Wycliffe reached no valuation of the papacy before the outbreak of the schism different from his later appraisal. If in his last years he identified the papacy with antichristianity, the dispensability of this papacy was strong in his mind before the schism.

For John Wycliffe, the Bible was the fundamental source of Christianity which is binding on all men. From this one can easily see how the next step came about: the furnishing of the Bible to the people in their mother tongue. Wycliffe was called "Doctor evangelicus" by his English and Bohemian followers. Of all the reformers who preceded Martin Luther, Wycliffe put most emphasis on Scripture: "Even though there were a hundred popes and though every mendicant monk were a cardinal, they would be entitled to confidence only in so far as they accorded with the Bible." Therefore in this early period it was Wycliffe who recognized and formulated the formal principle of the Reformation-- the unique authority of the Bible for the belief and life of the Christian.

Obviously Wycliffe was obsessed with his theories especially during his last years and probably made enemies of even his friends and maybe he should have eased off a bit on his attacks on the papacy but then that would have made him a mere mortal man and history books would have had no need to mention him. But certainly others took up the cause because of him and changes did come about but not to the extent of his wishes.

So there it is - The Reformation - in a nutshell, the reason why religion has become so diversified as to be barely unrecognizable from the original intent. Anyone reading this, of course will say, I could have told you that straight off, no need to write a book about it! But for my part I needed to go through history to get the whole story, (and my story is not complete yet) and to try and come to terms, not just with the diversity but especially with the violence. The Reformation was really a protest against the Catholic Church's power and parts of its doctrine, but why the formation of numerous different sects? Here is interpretation to suit individual needs again when what was required was getting back to basics and trying to understand what God really wanted and getting together as one people to achieve this goal. The Catholic Church could have used its superior position and leadership to provide the required changes but as history has shown the Catholic Church is concerned only with the Catholic Church and any changes that may result in a reduction of power and income just will not happen. More than any one sect, the Catholic Church has the most despicable record of violence, abusive tendencies and destruction of historical records and irreplaceable manuscripts on record going back two thousand years. It may be that there are now church institutions that rival the Catholic Church in membership numbers and a doctrine that is more sensible and practical to modern life but history cannot be re-written.

The Reformation, clearly was urgently required and resulted in religious sects being established but the minor theological differences between these new sects only subscribed to more questions and confusion and some newer sects can even be considered frivolous and unacceptable to some Christian scholars. Mention will only be made of the major churches appearing as a result of the Reformation but prior to that more comment on the most prominent reformers.

Martin Luther: From Bio. True Story - Born in Germany in 1483, Martin Luther became one of the most influential figures in Christian history when he began the Protestant Reformation in the 16th century. He called into question some of the basic tenets of Roman Catholicism, and his followers soon split from the Roman Catholic Church to begin the Protestant tradition.

The decision to become a monk was difficult and greatly disappointed his father, but he felt he must keep a promise. Luther was also driven by fears of hell and God's wrath, and felt that life in a monastery would help him find salvation. The first few years of monastery life were difficult for Martin Luther, as he did not find the religious enlightenment he was seeking. A mentor told him to focus his life exclusively on Christ and this would later provide him with the guidance he sought. At age 27, he was given the opportunity to be a delegate to a church conference in Rome. He came away more disillusioned, and very discouraged by the immorality and corruption he witnessed there among the Catholic priests. Finally, he realized the key to spiritual salvation was not to fear God or be enslaved by religious dogma but to believe that faith alone would bring salvation. This period marked a major change in his life and set in motion the Reformation. He eventually stated that he didn't consider the papacy had the authority to interpret scripture. The meeting ended in a shouting match and initiated his ultimate excommunication from the Church. From 1533 to his death in 1546, Martin Luther served as the dean of theology at University of Wittenberg. During this time he suffered from many illnesses, including arthritis, heart problems and digestive disorders, and the physical pain and emotional strain of being a fugitive might have been reflected in his writings. Some works contained strident and offensive language against several segments of society, particularly Jews and Muslims. During a trip to his hometown of Eisleben, he died on February 18, 1546, at age 62.

Legacy

Martin Luther is one of the most influential and controversial figures in the Reformation movement. His actions fractured the Roman Catholic Church into new sects of Christianity and set in motion reform within the Church. A prominent theologian, his desire for people to feel closer to God led him to translate the Bible into the language of the people, radically changing the relationship between church leaders and their followers.

Martin Luther, obviously carrying the torch lit originally by John Wycliffe and John Hus, is credited for introducing the type of Christianity known as Protestantism but the designation is now applied to most Western churches other than the Roman Catholic Church.

John Calvin (1509 AD – 1564 AD): Born July 10, in Noyon, France, Jean Calvin was raised in a staunch Roman Catholic family. The local bishop employed Calvin's father as an administrator in the town's cathedral. The father, in turn, wanted John to become a priest. Because of close ties with the bishop and his noble family, John's playmates and classmates in Noyon (and later in Paris) were aristocratic and culturally influential in his early life. The year 1534 was decisive for Calvin. From this time forward his influence became supreme, and all who had accepted the Reformed doctrines in France turned to him for counsel and instruction, attracted not only by his power as a teacher, but still more, perhaps because they saw in him so full a development of the Christian life according to the evangelical model. Calvin moved to Basel, Switzerland, where he was welcomed by the band of scholars and theologians who had conspired to make that city the Athens of Switzerland. There Calvin now gave himself to the study of Hebrew. When Calvin was 28, he moved again, to Geneva. Switzerland, and he stayed in Geneva, with the exception of a brief trip, for the rest of his life. In his later years, Calvin was afflicted with fever, asthma, and gout. In the early part of the year 1564 his sufferings became so severe that it was manifest his earthly career was rapidly drawing to a close. On. the 6th of February, 1564 John Calvin preached his last sermon, having with great difficulty found breath enough to carry him through it. He was several times after this carried to church, but never again was able to take any part in the service. He refused to receive his stipend, now that he was no longer able to discharge the duties of his office. In the midst of his sufferings, however, his zeal and energy kept him in continual occupation, as he commented, "Would you that the Lord should find me idle when He comes?"

With the possible exception of Martin Luther, no man has had a greater impact on the theology of the Protestant Churches today than John Calvin and his writing and preachings provided the seeds for the branch of theology that bears his name and the Reformed, Congregational, and Presbyterian churches, which look to Calvin as the chief expositor of their beliefs, have spread throughout the world.

Thomas Cranmer (1489 AD – 1556 AD): Briefly Cranmer was archbishop of Canterbury (1533 - 1556) and a leader of the English Reformation who was responsible for establishing the basic structures of the Church of England.

Thomas Cranmer entered the ministry for a simple reason: his father only had enough land to give his eldest son, so Thomas and his younger brother - as poor members of the gentry - joined the clergy. Cranmer was given a fellowship at Jesus College, Cambridge in 1510, which he lost when he married the daughter of a local tavern-keeper. She died in childbirth, at which point he was re-accepted by the college and devoted himself to study. He took holy orders in 1523. A plague forced Cranmer to leave Cambridge for Essex. Here, he came to the attention of King Henry VIII, who was staying nearby. The King found Cranmer a willing advocate for desired divorce from Catherine of Aragon. Cranmer argued the case as part of the embassy to Rome in 1530, and in 1532 became ambassador to Holy Roman Emperor Charles V. Cranmer was sent to Germany to learn more about the Lutheran movement, where he met Andreas Osiander, a Lutheran reformer whose ideology appealed to him. Osiander's niece also appealed to him, and Cranmer and the niece, Margaret, were married that year. Cranmer was becoming a Protestant… in the Kings Court! On March 30, 1533, he became Archbishop of Canterbury, and forced (for a time) to hide his married state. Once his appointment was approved by the Pope, Cranmer declared King Henry's marriage to Catherine void, and four months later married him to Anne Boleyn. In 1536 it was Anne Boleyn's marriage that was declared invalid, then Anne of Cleves 1540, then Catherine Howard. As King Henry divorces his many wives, Cranmer continued to be warmly supported by King Henry. Thomas Cranmer carefully danced around the politics of his position, and was able to push through the reforms that led gradually to the creation of the Church of England. Under the reign of Edward VI, Cranmer was allowed to make the doctrinal changes he thought necessary to the church. In 1549 he helped complete the Book of Common Prayer, for which his contributions are well-known.

After Edward VI's death, Thomas Cranmer supported Lady Jane Grey as successor. Her nine-day reign was followed by the Roman Catholic Queen "Bloody" Mary, who tried him for treason. After a long trial and imprisonment, he was forced to proclaim to the public his error in the support of Protestantism, an act designed to discourage followers of the religion. However, at his execution on March 21, 1556, he withdrew his forced confession, and proclaimed the truth of the Protestant faith. He placed his hand in the fire, the hand with which he had falsely signed his renouncement of his beliefs, and said, "**This hath offended!**" With that gesture, the government's hope of quelling the Protestant Reformation was lost.

From Wikipedia: When Elizabeth I came to power, she restored the Church of England's independence from Rome under the Elizabethan Religious Settlement. The church that she re-established was, in effect, a snapshot of the Edwardian Church from September 1552. Thus the Elizabethan Prayer Book was basically Cranmer's 1552 edition but without the "Black Rubric". In the Convocation of 1563, the **Forty-Two Articles** which were never adopted by the Church were altered in the area of eucharistic doctrine to form the **Thirty-Nine Articles**. Most of the exiles returned to England and resumed their careers in the Church. To some like Edmund Grindal, an Archbishop of Canterbury during Elizabeth's reign, Cranmer was a shining example whose work should be upheld and extended.

Cranmer's greatest concerns were the maintenance of the royal supremacy and the diffusion of reformed theology and practice. But he is best remembered for his contribution to the realm of language and of cultural identity. His prose helped to guide the development of the English language and the **Book of Common Prayer** is a major contribution to English literature that influenced many lives in the Anglophone world. It was the vehicle that guided Anglican worship for four hundred years. Catholic biographers sometimes depict Cranmer as an unprincipled opportunist, a Nicodemite and a tool of royal tyranny. For their part, hagiographic Protestant biographers sometimes overlook the times that Cranmer betrayed his own principles. Yet both sides can agree that Cranmer was a committed scholar whose life showed the strengths and weaknesses of a very human and often under-appreciated reformer. He is commemorated in the Anglican Communion as a Reformation Martyr on 21 March, the anniversary of his death.

John Wesley (1703 AD-1791 AD): In the 18th Century, a movement that came to be called "Methodism" began within the Church of England, led by discontented Anglican priests who believed the Church of England had become corrupt, effete, and too focused on the needs of the aristocracy. Methodism cast its lot with the working class, especially with the new industrial poor. Worship was simplified, new hymns were written, certain forms of abstinence became mandatory, and styles such as clergy vestments became less extravagant. From The Encyclopaedia Brittanica: **John Wesley,** (born June 17, 1703, Epworth, Lincolnshire, Eng.—died March 2, 1791, London), Anglican clergyman, evangelist, and founder, with his brother Charles, of the Methodist movement in the Church of England.

John Wesley was the second son of Samuel, a former Nonconformist (dissenter from the Church of England) and rector at Epworth, and Susanna Wesley. After six years of education at the Charterhouse, London, he entered Christ Church, Oxford University, in 1720. Graduating in 1724, he resolved to become ordained a priest; in 1725 he was made a deacon by the Bishop of Oxford and the following year was elected a fellow of Lincoln College. After assisting his father at Epworth and Wroot, he was ordained a priest on Sept. 22, 1728.

Recalled to Oxford in October 1729 to fulfill the residential requirements of his fellowship, John joined his brother Charles, Robert Kirkham, and William Morgan in a religious study group that was derisively called the "Methodists" because of their emphasis on methodical study and devotion. Taking over the leadership of the group from Charles, John helped the group to grow in numbers.

Wesley was a member of the Church of England until his death and would not schedule Methodist meetings to conflict with Anglican services. However, during the following fifty years John Wesley reportedly rode 250,000 miles on the roads of England, Scotland, and Ireland preaching 42,000 sermons. Besides this he published 233 books. His tireless and incessant activity changed the face of British society and the nature of its religion forever.

John Wesley was a powerful personality whose passion and devotion to his cause led him to explore and profoundly change people's views on Christianity. Throughout his life his eloquence, his determination and, sometimes, dictatorial nature enabled him to influence many people, so aiding the process of secularisation within the Church. Wesley's achievements spanned decades, his longevity enabling him to see Methodism's development from the first small societies at Lincoln College and Fetter Lane to the chapels of later years. He planted the seed of a new denomination, the Methodist Church, which was to grow and flourish in Britain and across the world for many years to come.

The following is worth getting an update on:

AN ANGLICAN-METHODIST COVENANT (interesting stuff from the internet):

Background:

The proposals for an Anglican Methodist Covenant, signed in November 2003, were developed during formal conversations which led to the publication of a **Common Statement** in December 2000.

This followed the work of a series of Informal Conversations held in 1995 and 1996 which identified a common understanding of the goal of visible unity.

The Common Statement sets down what the two churches agree in faith, their shared understanding of the nature of visible unity, mutual acknowledgements and commitments to each other and the identification of the next steps to be taken.

The Church of England and the Methodist Church already share a wide experience of working together locally, especially in Local Ecumenical Partnerships. During the Formal Conversations, the two churches focused particularly on how they can work together practically and grow together in fellowship in every place and at every level of each church's life.

Historical Context:

Ever since the time of John and Charles Wesley, there has been something ambiguous about the relationship between the Methodist Church and the Church of England.

The Wesleys founded an organisation which became a separate denomination. But they themselves remained priests in the Church of England until they died.

The relationship between the two churches since then, for more than two centuries, has been complex and constantly evolving:

"Anglican-Methodist separation may be seen as mutual estrangement which has changed both of us so that we cannot now think in terms of returning to where we were. Our culture as well as our theology and practice have developed independently and we will both need to move on if we are to find a new and common future. In this seeking of a new future, we need to bring our whole selves, past as well as present..." (Common Statement paragraph 42)

In the 1960s, in the context of the growing movement among all the Christian Churches to find visible unity, The Church of England and the Methodist Church of Great Britain negotiated proposals for union. Many from both Churches remember when these proposals failed to achieve the necessary two-thirds majority in the Church of England's General Synod. Work done since then, however, has provided a good foundation for today's Covenant.

"Disappointed hopes over the failure of earlier unity proposals have also left painful memories ... The healing of memories is a necessary part of the healing of the wounds of division in the body of Christ." (Common Statement paragraph 38)

"Our aim is not to put the clock back, but to gloss over differences, and to construct a monochrome unity. It is to harvest our diversity, to share our treasures and to remedy our shortcomings, so that we may enjoy together what we believe God has already given our churches and still holds in store for us." (Common Statement paragraph 42)

Conversations involving the United Reformed Church:

While the formal conversations were in progress, the Church of England and the Methodist Church were also involved in Informal Conversations with the United Reformed Church. These conversations began in 1999 and opened up exploration of the issues of eldership and conciliarity between the three churches.

These Informal Conversations also provided a vehicle of interaction between the United Reformed Church and the Formal Conversations between the Church of England and the Methodist Church.

I think a Covenant such as the above is wonderful, even though a long time coming. As I understand, there are minor (some would disagree) differences between say, Anglican, Reformed, Presbyterian, Congregational, Baptist and Methodist churches, mainly in their church services, selection of hymns and some forms of church government. With probably Anglicanism as the teaching and practice of the Church of England having greater differences than the others, being a sort of compromise (I apologise for this) with the Catholic Church. So my hope is that a Covenant will succeed possibly eventually encompassing all the above churches.

15
THE PRESENT
1900 AD to Present Day

The twentieth century (and now into the twenty first), like many other centuries was very eventful. There were two world wars, World War 1 was called the war to end all wars – that was wishful thinking – and then World War 2 – what should that one be called? So many lives lost and yet as some historians and statisticians will say, sometimes calamities help in keeping the population growth in check eg. The Black Death in the Middle Ages. At least none of these catastrophic events could be considered 'religious wars'.

We've put a man on the moon and brought him back, we've more knowledge of the planets in our solar system and we seem very close to understanding the origin of the universe and yet we still have serious religious conflict in the very land where God first gave us hope. The insane violence between rival Muslim sects, notably the Shiites and the Sunnis, stems from a family feud going back to the seventh century as to who should succeed the prophet Mohammed, himself deemed a representative of our One God! Is this to be believed, really? We should be thankful that Muslims, for the most part, avoided Christianity's decades-long battles that occurred after the crusades. But not only has that to be resolved, there is a continuing interference from those cowboys in the USA with their stetsons flying ant their six-guns blazing intent on changing the world, making it in their image you might say (or more likely there is a promise of financial reward). In actual fact when the USA invaded Iraq, a relative calm that existed between the

Shiites and the Sunnis at that time was blown apart, stripping power from one sect and igniting sectarian violence that has resulted in tens of thousands of deaths and this violence continues to this day. Of course now it's difficult to differentiate the religious from the political aspects of the Middle East, but the clerics on both sides of these Muslim sects make a point of stirring up the pot whenever they can.

Halliday, Fred, 100 myths about the Middle East

The problem with Islam is that it is in need of a 'Reformation'

" This injunction, repeated by some Muslim reformers as well as Western observers, confuses several issues. First of all, if by 'Reformation' is meant a period of debate, rational discussion of religion and the rejection of a single religious authority such as the Vatican, then Islam has long exhibited such tendencies. Islam, without a Vatican, has no concept of heresy. There never was, after 661 AD and the division between Sunni and Shi'i, a single authority, and there is not even a formal religious hierarchy as in Christianity.

If by 'Reformation' is meant religious thinking freed of dogmatism, then the history of Islamic thought has long been characterised by rationalist and open trends, notably that of the Mu'tazilis (eighth and ninth centuries AD), who criticised dogmatic thinking and were supported by Caliph al-Mamun in 827 AD and the Andalusian philosopher Ibn 'Arabi (died 1273). For centuries Muslim thinkers, largely but not only Shi'is, have practised what is termed ijtihad, independent and critical interpretation of sacred texts and traditions. More recently, in the twentieth century, there have been many Muslim thinkers who have reviewed, in an open and critical spirit, the claims and interpretation of Islam.

However, this call for a 'Reformation' also misrepresents other issues. On one hand it ascribes to the Protestantism that followed the Reformation a freedom of spirit and a tolerance of secular debate that is markedly absent from much of today's Protestantism, as is evident in the fervent intolerance of the US. On the other hand, and most importantly, it confuses cause and effect: Arab society and much of the Muslim world

119

are not dictatorial, authoritarian or intellectually paralysed because of religion, but the other way around - it is the existence, for other reasons, of such states and societies that itself produces a paralysed religion. The solution to censorship in the Arab world, for example, or the inequality of women, is not to be found in changing religious doctrine or interpretation, but in changing society and the state themselves. For its part, Islam is capable of greater theological flexibility, starting from the principle - which is available for use by those who so choose - that the verses of the Qur'an, instead of being one block of unchallengeable dogma, divide into those which are nasikh (i.e. which prevail), and those which are mansukh (i.e. prevailed over). To most Muslims, for example, verses on stoning criminals to death or on slavery are, in the contemporary world, mansukh.

The three monotheistic religious communities called Judaism, Christianity and Islam now constitute the single largest block of organized believers on earth. To unify them under the name of monotheists is merely to begin to describe the ties that bind them. All worship what we may identify, with reservations, as the same God. All three believe this deity has intervened in human history on several occasions. Besides sharing a vast array of ideology, history and traditions, each of the three communities traces itself back to a sacred Scripture – Muslims properly call them People of the Book – a book that each believes was revealed by The One True God that they all worship. All three may be called "Abrahamic" in the sense that there is an Abraham story at the heart of their long term memory and each thinks that it is the unique beneficiary of the promise of being the sole genuine heir among Abraham's children. The basis of Islam and Muhammad's message was that he was advocating a new call to Monotheism calling it "the new religion of Abraham"

As the Quran argues, Abraham was before Moses and Torah and before Jesus and the Gospel so he cannot be regarded as either a Jew or a Christian but the Quran's claim to affinity to Abraham was in effect a denial of dependence on, or derivation from, either Judaism or Christianity but that prideful link to Abraham had, at the same time, made Islam a brother to both of the other two. Together they were, and are, siblings in the family of Abraham.

It is not easy to chart the interconfessional passage of believers from one faith community to another but it has been noted that that almost all the early converts to Christianity were Jews or Jewish satellite believers or Jewish sympathizers and that once Islam got past the pagan Bedouin of Arabia, the overwhelming number of new Muslims were made out of the ranks of the Jews and the Christians. Like modern fundamentalists, ancient monotheists were chiefly bent on converting each other."

Other significant events in the twentieth century: (in the Middle East):

1917 – Four hundred years of Ottoman rule was ended by British conquest. The Ottoman Empire was an imperial state that was founded in 1299 and was an empire inspired and sustained by Islam, and Islamic institutions after growing out of the break-down of several Turkish tribes. The empire then grew to include many areas in what is now present-day Europe to and it eventually became one of the largest, most powerful and longest-lasting empires in the history of the world. At its peak the Ottoman Empire included the areas of Turkey, Egypt, Greece, Bulgaria, Romania, Macedonia, Hungary, Israel, Jordan, Lebanon, Syria, and parts of the Arabian Peninsula and North Africa. It had a maximum area of 7.6 million square miles (19.9 million square kilometers) in 1595 (University of Michigan). The Ottoman Empire began to decline power in the 18th century but a portion of its land became what is Turkey today.

The 19th century saw medieval backwardness gradually give way to the first signs of progress, with various Western powers jockeyed for position, often through missionary activities. British, French and American scholars launched studies of biblical geography and archeology; Britain, France, Russia, Austria and the United States opened consulates in Jerusalem. Steamships began to ply regular routes between the Land and Europe; postal and telegraphic connections were installed; the first road was built connecting Jerusalem and Jaffa. The Land's rebirth as a crossroads for commerce of three continents was accelerated by the opening of the Suez Canal.

Consequently, the condition of the country's Jews slowly improved, and their numbers increased substantially. By mid-century, overcrowded conditions within the walled city of Jerusalem motivated the Jews to build the first neighborhood outside the walls (1860) and, in the next quarter century, to add seven more, forming the nucleus of the New City. By 1880, Jerusalem had an overall Jewish majority. Land for farming was purchased throughout the country; new rural settlements were set up; and the Hebrew language, long restricted to liturgy and literature, was revived. The stage was being set for the founding of the Zionist movement. British Foreign Minister Balfour pledged support for establishment of a "Jewish national home in Palestine". (Nothing more worthless than a politician's promise)

1918-1948 – British Rule - The Great war was to unexpectedly turn the imperial spotlight onto this part of the world. As the Ottomans had thrown in their hand with the Germans, it was inevitable that the British would want to defend their strategic connection with India through the Suez. And, in 1915 they would even try to force a way through to the Russians through the Dardanelles. Palestine was suddenly thrust into an active theatre of war. At this period of time the most important indigenous group that the British had to work with was the Arabs. The number of Jews in Palestine were less than 60,000 at the outbreak of the war. Therefore, initial British contacts were, almost exclusively, aimed at the Arabs. The most important advance at this time was when the British High Commissioner of Egypt, Sir Henry McMahon, tried to co-opt the help of the Sharif of Mecca, in the fight against the Ottomans. He did this through a series of correspondence known as the Hussein-McMahon letters. This correspondence seemed to promise the Arabs their own state stretching from Damascus to the Arabian peninsular in return for fighting the Ottomans. However, not only was the correspondence deliberately imprecise but the status and ability of the Sharif of Mecca to speak for all of the Arabs was itself in question. Despite these problems, the Sharif of Mecca formally declared a revolt against Ottoman rule in 1916. Britain provided supplies and money for the Arab forces led by the Sharif's sons; Abdullah and Faisal. British military advisers were also detailed from Cairo to assist the Arab army that the brothers were organizing. Of these advisers, <u>T.E. Lawrence</u> was to become the best known.

In 1918 the British captured Palestine from the Ottoman Turks. They planned to include Palestine as a colony of the British Empire. The British aimed to establish a foothold in the Middle East and advance their interests in the region, specifically vis-a-vis the oil fields of the area. The British Mandate for Palestine began at a time of rising nationalism, both among the Arabs and the Jews of Palestine. The British policy was to appease the Arabs and the Jews of Tzfat suffered. The Arab-Jewish town of Tzfat or <u>Safed</u> was a key player in the events of the era and the British were hard-pressed to keep order in the city.

Following the fall of the Ottoman-Turkish Empire, the British assumed the role of Palestine's government. The British Mandate for Palestine formalized British rule over Palestine and voiced the British government's favorable view of the eventual establishment of a national home for the Jewish people in Palestine.

This was greeted with great excitement and anticipation by the Jews of Palestine, including Tzfat's Jews. The city had suffered greatly under Turkish rule and the prospect of a benevolent government brought a sigh of relief. Even more importantly, many of Tzfat's Jews were active in the Zionist movement and planned for the day when they would be able to establish an independent Jewish country. Along with the new Zionist movement, the community in Safed was split regarding other new innovations and institutions. The city did not have a central town council; rather communal decisions were made by rabbis. The older religious residents opposed attempts to introduce new educational systems. Baron Rothchild's donations towards establishing a modern Hebrew public school were rebuffed by the establishment and when the school opened, the Ashkanazi families refused to enroll their children.

The new Zionist ideology made inroads into the traditional community in Tzfat. Many young people abandoned the Orthodoxy of their parents to follow a more "modern" path. Young singles and families also moved out of Tzfat to new agricultural settlements nearby including settlements of Rosh Pinna, Mishmar Hayarden, Metulla and Yesod HaMala.

In addition to its importance in the general history of the British Empire, the Palestine Mandate represents an interesting case study of

British Imperialism in practice during the twentieth century. Some aspects of Palestine were unique, particularly the Balfour Declaration's promise to assist in the creation of a "National Home" for the Jewish people in Palestine without dispossessing local Arabs which placed the British in the middle of a conflict between Palestinian Arabs and Zionists. London never settled on a policy that made both the Jews and the Arabs happy.

However, in some ways Palestine shared features of other parts of the Empire. While the Mandate was a responsibility given to Britain by the League of Nations it was run essentially like a Crown Colony with no local assembly and all important posts held by British nationals. Britain's interest in Palestine served a strategic purpose due to its strategic location near the Middle East's oil field and the Suez Canal. Another imperial feature common to Palestine was the practice of British colonial officials to informally divide indigenous populations into "good" and "bad" groups. In Palestine the Arabs (romanticized as courageous Bedouin tribesmen) were the "good" locals, while the Jewish Zionists (whom the British characterized as pushy and grasping) made up the "bad" element. Of course, both groups were considered inferior by the British and in need of the aid of an advanced nation.

Palestine fell into British hands in December 1917 when General Allenby captured Jerusalem from the Turks. The first task of the occupying forces was to provide food for the impoverished residents of Palestine who had suffered neglect at the hands of the Ottomans. Wartime occupation turned to formal responsibility in 1920 when the League of Nations granted authority in Palestine to Britain until the territory was deemed fit for self-rule. Despite the Balfour Declaration, and the official Mandate policy of establishing a homeland for the Jews, the Jewish community joined the Arabs in mistrusting their new rulers.

London's policy of promoting Zionism worried the British officials in Palestine. Humphrey Bowan, Mandate Director of Education, noted in his diary that "It is indeed difficult to see how we can keep our promise to the Jews ... without inflicting injury on nine-tenths of the population". London, however, still clung to the conflicting ideas of creating a Jewish homeland and keeping the Arab population content.

The intense rivalry and competition between the Jews and Arabs was to afflict the British administration for virtually their entire period of governance. Unfortunately, the Zionists and the Arabs had mutually exclusive goals. The Zionists wished to create a Jewish homeland in their Holy Land. Whereas the Arabs were equally adamant that they should not lose their autonomy and rights in their own homeland. At this stage, the Arabs still massively formed the majority of the population. But what the Zionists lacked in numbers they more than made up for with political influence in the West and a zeal to succeed that bordered on fanaticism.

The fact that the British mandate included references to the Balfour Declaration and the establishment of a Jewish homeland was a severe blow to the Arabs. Partly to try and mollify this disappointment, the British split the Palestine mandate into two distinct areas, using the Jordan River as a natural boundary. The British claimed that Jewish immigration would be confined to the West of the river. The East of the river, which represented three quarters of the whole mandate area was to be reserved for the Arabs alone. The Hashemite Abdulla was to become the ruler of what was to become Transjordan. Most Arabs still felt ill at ease with this British plan. They regarded Transjordan as little more than an arid, empty desert. Besides, the principle of any Jewish homeland anywhere in Arab lands was still completely abhorrent to them.

Arab intransigence and unwillingness to work with the Jews was demonstrated almost immediately as the British tried to set up a legislative council and a constitution. The council was supposed to have ten of the seats allocated to the Arabs and only two to the Jews. The Arabs refused to cooperate on the basis that two seats for so few Jews meant that they were relatively over represented. They also resented the comments and concessions made to Zionism in the constitution. This failure meant that the British had no choice but to continue ruling Palestine directly themselves.

Over the next few years, the British made repeated attempts to include both communities in the day to day running of the mandate. Time and time again, Arab intransigence resulted in an absolute refusal to cooperate in any way. Conversely, the Jews were happy to work and cooperate with the authorities and thus gained a legitimacy and administrative experience far and above that which the size of their community merited. The best example of this was the creation of a Jewish agency in 1929. Arabs flatly refused to do the same.

In fact, 1929 saw the birth of the first real instance of communal ugliness. It would set off a trend that would keep rearing its ugly head for nearly as long as the British were in control of the mandate. The Wailing Wall incident was when Arabs and Jews clashed over a stretch of wall that was regarded as religiously important to both religions. Arabs tried to make access to this wall for the Jews as awkward and difficult as possible. In the end, fights broke out which flared into riots around the country. Some 133 Jews were killed (mostly by British authorities) and 116 Arabs died.

London's response to the rioting was to issue a White Paper in October 1930 which stipulated that further Jewish immigration would be limited by the ability of Palestine's economy to absorb them. The Arab community was not placated by these changes and when the policy was revised in February 1931 to be more favorable to Zionism the Arabs were outraged. The problem became more acute when Zionism was given a boost by the rise to power of the Nazi Party. Thousands of German Jews fled to Palestine to avoid persecution. Arab unhappiness with Zionism and British rule led to a full-scale revolt by Palestinian Arabs in 1936. While the Arab Revolt was defeated with harsh military measures, conciliation was soon offered to the Arab community. With war approaching in Europe, Whitehall wanted to insure Arab loyalty. London assumed that Jews would be anti-fascist regardless of British policy in Palestine. A new White Paper issued in May 1939 called for the eventual creation of an independent Palestine containing both Jews and Arabs, although the size of the Jewish population would be limited. Jewish immigration would be capped at 75,000 people for the next five years, after which any further influx would have to be approved by the Arabs.

During World War II, Palestine was relatively peaceful compared to the rest of the Middle East. However, problems still mounted for the

Mandate government. There was a flood of Jewish refugees arriving from Germany, Poland, and Romania, with Zionist assistance, despite the best efforts of the British to keep to the limits set by the 1939 White Paper. In a sinister development, the number of refugees only declined in 1942 when the Nazis decided to implement the "Final Solution" and therefore stopped the refugees from leaving Axis territory. While the Jewish community was upset that the British authorities were not permitting more refugees to enter Palestine, the threat of a German victory in North Africa kept most Zionists cooperating with the British. In return for the support of the Jewish Agency, the mainstream Jewish defense force, the Haganah, was allowed to arm and train in contravention of the law, as long as they were discreet. On the other hand, the more extreme Zionists and their military organizations, the Irgun and the so-called Stern Gang, advocated the immediate creation of a Jewish State. As the war drew to a close the Haganah joined the Irgun and the Stern Gang in launching attacks on the British.

Sympathy for the plight of Europe's Jews during the war did not override the anti-Zionist stance of most Mandate officials who worked hard to keep out illegal refugees. When the cooperation between the Zionists and the Mandate authorities turned to violence near the end of the war, the British attitude toward the Jews hardened even more.

Jewish hopes rose when the war ended and the Labour Party came to power, but Foreign Secretary Ernest Bevin did not prove to be the ally that the Zionists expected. Anxious to avoid angering its valuable Arab allies, London refused to allow large-scale resettlement of Jewish refugees to Palestine and opposed the creation of a Jewish State. With no support for their aims forthcoming from London, the various Zionist military formations began an active terrorist campaign to drive the British from Palestine. Illegal immigration of Jewish refugees to Palestine, with the active support of the Jewish community in the Mandate, increased dramatically. Assassinations, attacks on police and military bases, bombings, and sabotage increased during 1946. One of the most spectacular attacks was the Irgun's bombing of the King David Hotel in July 1946. Designed to destroy the wing of the hotel which housed the offices of the Palestine Administration, the blast killed over ninety people, Britons, Jews, and Arabs alike. British authorities could not quell the violence despite deploying 100,000 police and soldiers, and the security forces increasingly withdrew into fortified camps mockingly dubbed "Bevingrads" by the Jews. The situation became so dangerous that in early 1947 non-essential personnel were evacuated by the British.

By this time the British public was tired of the bloody, and seemingly pointless, war in Palestine. The Truman Administration's support for the partition of Palestine further undercut London's desire to retain the Mandate. In late 1947, after the UN General Assembly approved a plan to divide Palestine into separate Jewish and Arab states, the British announced that they would end their administration of the Mandate on May 15, 1948. The last few months of British rule in Palestine saw a steady deterioration of public services and security as troops and administrators were withdrawn. The United Nations had not sent an adequate organization to replace the British and Palestine fell into civil war. The "scuttle" from Palestine was not a proud moment for the British Empire. "Withdrawing without designating a successor, the British had not so much transferred power as abandoned it," it was concluded.

After the Second World War ended Jewish efforts to secure independence increased. Both the Jews and the Arabs eyed Safed as an important military target and prepared for eventual battle. When the United Nations voted to end the British Mandate and allow the Jews to create their own nation, both sides began to prepare to liberate Tzfat, each for their own cause.

In 1946, shortly before the British left Tzfat, they estimated that the Jewish population of the city was 2,400 and the Muslim population was 9780, with an additional 430 Christian Arabs living in the Arab Quarter. Tzfat or Safed is one of the four holy cities in Israel, together with Jerusalem, Hebron and Tiberias. The old part of town consists of narrow cobblestone alleys revealing artists' galleries, medieval synagogues, private homes and small guest houses. Despite its small population (ca 27,000), Safed is once again making its mark on the map.

The United Nations plan came to nothing. The British left Palestine in May 1948 and the Jews set up Israel almost immediately using territory given to them in the United Nations plan.

Active warfare commenced immediately after the UN Partition Resolution of 29 November 1947, and before the British departure. The Arab Higher Committee called a general strike and local Arab militias attacked Jewish settlements, Jewish quarters in the cities and Jewish buses.

Have we learned nothing? Or is this area doomed for eternity to follow the same destructive path that it has followed for five thousand years? Surely now is the time for a message from God! Can these people even spell the word religion? I doubt if they can spell the word 'God'!

The UK and the US imposed an arms embargo on Palestine, but the British continued to supply weapons to Trans-Jordan and Iraq. The Jewish forces smuggled arms from Yugoslavia and Czechoslovakia, since at this time they still had support from the Communist bloc.

In January 1948 Fauzi al Kaukji, who had joined the Mufti in Germany during the world war, led the Arab Liberation Army across the border from Lebanon, attacked towns and settlements in the north of the country and moved south towards Tel Aviv, and the Arab Higher Committee operated in the centre. By March 1948 Arab forces had cut the road to Jerusalem, which was later bombarded by the artillery of the Trans-Jordanian Arab Legion, commanded by the British Lieutenant-General Sir John Bagot Glubb.

It was at this time that 245 civilians were killed by the Irgun forces at Deir Yassin, an Arab village near Jerusalem. The Arab media accused the Jewish force of a calculated massacre, while the Irgun leadership claimed that the deaths occurred in the heat of battle and after loudspeaker warnings to evacuate. The action was condemned by the Jewish government and the responsible officers were arrested. The Arab media story precipitated widespread panic among the Arab inhabitants of the region, and it still remains a central feature of Arab accounts of the period.

Shortly afterwards a medical convoy to the hospital in Jerusalem was ambushed by Arab forces and 77 medical personnel were killed. In May 1948, immediately before Israel's independence, the Arab Legion captured a group of Jewish villages, known as the "Etzion bloc", immediately to the south of Jerusalem, but outside the proposed Jewish state, and 127 inhabitants and defenders were killed by machine guns and grenades after they surrendered.

The last few paragraphs are purely political history but are relevant to the story as showing the turmoil that existed (and exists) in the Holy Land, with attempts by the Western world to provide a solution. A solution, by the way, that would benefit greatly the likes of Great Britain and its allies.

Doesn't it seem like this road has been travelled before? Present day Israel, not content with the land and boundaries that were offered by the United Nations in 1948 (whether a fair assessment or not is irrelevant at this stage), had no intention of staying within those boundaries and with much superior armed forces than the surrounding Arab peoples had already decided to take what Israel appears to assume is rightfully theirs. It was not their land in 1250 BC but it did not stop them from taking it by force (as the Bible explains), and expanding their conquests and dividing the area up into tribal segments before eventually losing control and being dispersed to the far corners of the known world at that time. Israel did forfeit all claims to the land and were allowed to return to Jerusalem only with certain conditions and permissions. Over the years it was not just Jews who migrated back to the area but many other nations, the difference being the Jews maintained their clan ties and religion and grew together as a nation but without a home.

It is not the intention to pursue the Middle East problems further (that discussion may come at a later date), but a word about Palestine. The name Palestine originates from Roman times and was approximately the Biblical Land of Canaan (isn't that ironical!), but the boundaries have varied over the years and at the time of the British Mandate, covered all of Jordan and what is now Israel and the territories between them. It is considered a State by most Arab countries but obviously not be Israel. Palestine has applied for United Nations status and recognition. That

Great Britain walked away from its mandate is absolutely criminal but no less criminal than the United States supplying financial aid and arms to Israel when at the time of the decision to form the State of Israel and provide a homeland for the Jews, most western countries including the United States were against this resolution. Is there a place for God in all this? I don't think so.

The Arab or Palestine reaction to the decision to take away a good portion of their land, homes and businesses and give it to the Jews is understandable and which actually resulted in many thousands being displaced to accommodate this so called solution, not to mention the ongoing death and destruction. They were the victims once before and they are determined that they will not be victims again but until the playing field is levelled they will be the victims. God seems to be on the side of the People of Israel again, only this time God is flying an F18.

CONCLUSION

It is fitting that the story should end as it began, with the Jewish people and the historic religion of Judaism, not only is the Jewish religion's integrity at stake here at this time but also Islam and Christianity, all three of the Abrahamic religions. There is no desire to get drawn into the specifics of the current Middle East conflict, suffice to say that it is horrendous by any Era's standards and is obviously not what God would have wanted. There is no bias one way or the other so I have taken the liberty of borrowing a couple of passages which plainly describe the difficulties of attaining peace between Arabs and Jews which at this time is possibly as far back as it ever was.

Alison Weir "If America Knew"

CounterPunch & **AntiWar.com** (The Real Story of How Israel was Created) October 11, 2011

To better understand the Palestinian bid for membership in the United Nations, it is important to understand the original 1947 UN action on Israel-Palestine. The common representation of Israel's birth is that the UN created Israel, that the world was in favor of this move, and that the US governmental establishment supported it. All these assumptions are demonstrably incorrect. In reality, while the UN General Assembly recommended the creation of a Jewish state in part of Palestine, that recommendation was non-binding and never implemented by the Security Council.

Second, the General Assembly passed that recommendation only after Israel proponents threatened and bribed numerous countries in order to gain a required two-thirds of votes.

Third, the US administration supported the recommendation out of domestic electoral considerations, and took this position over the strenuous objections of the State Department, the CIA, and the Pentagon.

The passage of the General Assembly recommendation sparked increased violence in the region. Over the following months the armed wing of the pro-Israel movement, which had long been preparing for war, perpetrated a series of massacres and expulsions throughout Palestine, implementing a plan to clear the way for a majority-Jewish state.

It was this armed aggression, and the ethnic cleansing of at least three-quarters of a million indigenous Palestinians, that created the Jewish state on land that had been 95 percent non-Jewish prior to Zionist immigration and that even after years of immigration remained 70 percent non-Jewish. And despite the shallow patina of legality its partisans extracted from the General Assembly, Israel was born over the opposition of American experts and of governments around the world, who opposed it on both pragmatic and moral grounds.

Let us look at the specifics.

Background of the UN partition recommendation

In 1947 the UN took up the question of Palestine, a territory that was then administered by the British.

Approximately 50 years before, a movement called political Zionism had begun in Europe. Its intention was to create a Jewish state in Palestine through pushing out the Christian and Muslim inhabitants who made up over 95 percent of its population and replacing them with Jewish immigrants.

As this colonial project grew through subsequent years, the indigenous Palestinians reacted with occasional bouts of violence; Zionists had anticipated this since people usually resist being expelled from their land. In various written documents cited by numerous Palestinian and Israeli historians, they discussed their strategy: they would buy up the land until all the previous inhabitants had emigrated, or, failing this, use violence to force them out.

When the buy-out effort was able to obtain only a few percent of the land, Zionists created a number of terrorist groups to fight against both the Palestinians and the British. Terrorist and future Israeli Prime Minister Menachem Begin later bragged that Zionists had brought terrorism both to the Middle East and to the world at large.

Finally, in 1947 the British announced that they would be ending their control of Palestine, which had been created through the League of Nations following World War One, and turned the question of Palestine over to the United Nations.

At this time, the Zionist immigration and buyout project had increased the Jewish population of Palestine to 30 percent and land ownership from 1 percent to approximately 6 percent. Since a founding principle of the UN was "self-determination of peoples," one would have expected to the UN to support fair, democratic elections in which inhabitants could create their own independent country. Instead, Zionists pushed for a General Assembly resolution in which they would be given a disproportionate 55 percent of Palestine. (While they rarely announced this publicly, their stated plan was to later take the rest of Palestine.)

How Palestine became Israel: If Americans Knew Last Updated April 2013

In the late 1800s a small, fanatic movement called "political Zionism" began in Europe. Its goal was to create a Jewish state somewhere in the world. Its leaders settled on the ancient and long-inhabited land of Palestine for the location of this state.

Palestine's population at this time was approximately ninety-six percent non-Jewish (primarily Muslim and Christian). Over the coming decades Zionist leaders used various strategies to accomplish their goal of taking over Palestine:

Encouraging Jewish immigration to Palestine, partly through the invention of such deceptive slogans as "a land without a people for a people without a land," when, in fact, the land was already inhabited. Since the majority of Jews were not Zionists until after WWII, Zionists used an array of misleading strategies, including secret collaboration with the Nazis, to push immigration.

Convincing a "Great Power" to back this process. By turn, Zionists approached the Ottomans, the British, and the U.S. to further their cause. While the Ottomans turned them down, the British (being promised that American Zionists would push the U.S. to enter World War I on the side of England) eventually acceded, as did the U.S. (due to concerns of politicians like Harry Truman that they would lose elections otherwise).

Buying up the land (sometimes through subterfuges), proclaiming it Jewish for all eternity, and refusing to allow non-Jews to live or work on the purchased land. This was called "redeeming" the land and was financed by a variety of means, including by such wealthy banking families as the Rothschilds.

Historic Palestine, the land now occupied by the State of Israel, was a multicultural society. During the 1947-49 war, Israel committed at least 33 massacres and expelled over 750,000 Palestinians.

In the 1930s, Jewish land ownership had increased from approximately 1% to just over 6% of the land, and violence had increased as well. With the emergence of several Zionist terrorist gangs (whose ranks included a number of future Prime Ministers of Israel), there was violent conflict. Numerous people of all ethnicities were killed – then, as now, the large majority of them Christian and Muslim Palestinians.

The Catastrophe

This growing violence culminated in Israel's ruthless 1947-49 "War of Independence," in which at least 750,000 Palestinian men, women, and children were expelled from their homes by numerically superior Israeli forces – half before any Arab armies joined the war. This massive humanitarian disaster is known as 'The Catastrophe,' al Nakba in Arabic.

Zionist forces committed 33 massacres and destroyed 531 Palestinian towns. Author Norman Finkelstein states: "According to the former director of the Israeli army archives, 'in almost every village occupied by us during the War... acts were committed which are defined as war crimes, such as murders, massacres, and rapes'...Uri Milstein, the authoritative Israeli military historian of the 1948 war, goes one step further, maintaining that 'every skirmish ended in a massacre of Arabs.'

Count Folke Bernadotte, a former official of the Swedish Red Cross who saved thousands of Jews during World War II and was appointed U.N. mediator in Palestine, said of the refugees: "It would be an offence against the principles of elemental justice if these innocent victims of the conflict were denied the right to return to their homes." Bernadotte was assassinated by a Zionist organization led by future Israeli Prime Minister Yitzhak Shamir.

Injustice Continues

Over the 60 years since Israel's founding on May 14, 1948, this profound injustice has continued. Palestinian refugees are the largest remaining refugee population in the world.

1.3 million Palestinians live in Israel as "Israeli citizens," but despite their status as citizens, they are subject to systematic discrimination. Many are prohibited from living in the villages and homes from which they were violently expelled, and their property has been confiscated for Jewish-only uses. In Orwellian terminology, Israeli law designates these internal refugees as "present absentees."

In 1967 Israel launched its third war and seized still more Palestinian (and other Arab) land. Israel also attacked a U.S. Navy ship, the USS Liberty, killing and injuring over 200 Americans, an event that remains largely covered-up today, despite efforts by an extraordinary array of high-level military officers and civilian officials to expose it.

Israel occupied the West Bank and Gaza Strip – the final 22% of mandatory Palestine – and began building settlements for Jewish Israelis on land confiscated from Palestinian Muslims and Christians. It has demolished more than 24,145 Palestinian homes since 1967. In 2005 Israel returned Gazan land to its owners, but continues to control its borders, ports, and air space, turning Gaza into a large prison, where 1.5 million people are held under what a UN Human Rights Commissioner described as "catastrophic" conditions.

Over 7,000 Palestinian men, women, and children are imprisoned in Israeli jails under physically abusive conditions (many have not even been charged with a crime) and the basic human rights of all Palestinians under Israeli rule are routinely violated. Some prisoners tortured by Israel have been American citizens. In the violence that began in fall, 2000 through Feb. 5, 2009, Israeli forces killed 6,348 Palestinians; Palestinian resistance groups killed 1,072 Israelis. Israel's military, the fourth most powerful on earth possesses hundreds of nuclear weapons.

American Involvement

American taxpayers give Israel more than $8 million per day, even though surveys reveal that 73% of Americans oppose taking sides on Israel-Palestine. Because of Israel's powerful US lobby, Congress gives far more money to Israel than to all of sub-Saharan Africa put together. In its 60 years of existence, Israel, the size of New Jersey, has received more U.S. tax money than any other nation. While most Americans are unaware of these facts (studies have shown that media report on Israeli deaths at rates up to 13 times greater than they report on Palestinian deaths) governmental actions are making Americans responsible for a continuing catastrophe of historic proportions – and which is, in addition, creating extremely damaging enmity to the US itself. Israel partisans have played a significant role in promoting U.S. attacks on Iraq and Iran.

From Jewish history and perspective:

Active warfare commenced immediately after the UN Partition Resolution of 29 November 1947, and before the British departure. The Arab Higher Committee called a general strike and local Arab militias attacked Jewish settlements, Jewish quarters in the cities and Jewish buses.

The UK and the US imposed an arms embargo on Palestine, but the British continued to supply weapons to Trans-Jordan and Iraq. The Jewish forces smuggled arms from Yugoslavia and Czechoslovakia, since at this time they still had support from the Communist bloc.

In January 1948 Fauzi al Kaukji, who had joined the Mufti in Germany during the world war, led the Arab Liberation Army across the border from Lebanon, attacked towns and settlements in the north of the country and moved south towards Tel Aviv, and the Arab Higher Committee operated in the centre. By March 1948 Arab forces had cut the road to Jerusalem, which was later bombarded by the artillery of the Trans-Jordanian Arab Legion, commanded by the British Lieutenant-General Sir John Bagot Glubb.

It was at this time that 245 civilians were killed by the Irgun forces at Deir Yassin, an Arab village near Jerusalem. The Arab media accused the Jewish force of a calculated massacre, while the Irgun leadership claimed that the deaths occurred in the heat of battle and after loudspeaker warnings to evacuate. The action was condemned by the Jewish government and the responsible officers were arrested. The Arab media story precipitated widespread panic among the Arab inhabitants of the region, and it still remains a central feature of Arab accounts of the period.

Shortly afterwards a medical convoy to the hospital in Jerusalem was ambushed by Arab forces and 77 medical personnel were killed. In May 1948, immediately before Israel's independence, the Arab Legion captured a group of Jewish villages, known as the "Etzion bloc", immediately to the south of Jerusalem, but outside the proposed Jewish state, and 127 inhabitants and defenders were killed by machine guns and grenades after they surrendered. In the Security Council, immediately before the British withdrawal, the United States proposed a cease fire and the postponement of Israel's independence. The US proposal was rejected by the Jewish Provisional Council of State by six votes to four, at a time when the outcome of the expected war was greatly in doubt.

On 14th May 1948 the British Mandate ended and Israel proclaimed its independence as a sovereign state within the borders determined by the United Nations Partition Resolution of 29 November 1947. A Provisional Government was established under the leadership of David Ben Gurion as Prime Minister. The Arab nations rejected the Partition Resolution, as they denied the legitimacy of Jewish settlement in Palestine. The Arabs of Palestine therefore refused to establish an Arab state in the area contemplated by the Partition Resolution, since this would imply recognition of a Jewish state in the remaining part of Palestine.

On the first night of Israel's independence Tel Aviv was bombed by Egyptian planes. On 15 May 1948, the Egyptian Foreign Minister informed the Security Council that "Egyptian armed forces have started to enter Palestine to establish law and order" (cable to the Security Council, S/743 15 May 1948). During that night the regular armies of Egypt, Syria, Transjordan, Lebanon and Iraq, supported by volunteers from Sudan and Saudi Arabia invaded Israel. Azzam Pasha, Secretary-General of the Arab League, announced:

"This will be a war of extermination and a momentous massacre which will be spoken of like the Mongolian massacre and the Crusades."

When the conflict began, the Jewish forces numbered some 36,500, and were without tanks, heavy weapons or combat aircraft."

After initial Arab successes, the Jewish forces recaptured some territory. Count Folke Bernadotte of Sweden was appointed as a mediator by the United Nations, and he negotiated a truce which came into effect on 11 June 1948.

During the four weeks of the truce, Israel received an airlift of arms from Czechoslovakia, which was then a satellite of the Soviet Union. After 7 July 1948 there were ten days of fierce fighting in which Israeli forces opened a corridor to Jerusalem, and took Upper Galilee in the north and Beersheba in the south. On 17th July1948 the Security Council imposed a further cease-fire, supported by threat of sanctions against Israel. Bernadotte then proposed a peace plan, which included a reduced area for Israel in "union" with an enlarged Kingdom of Transjordan, and an Arab administration of Jerusalem. Jewish immigration would be unlimited for a period of two years and after that it would then be subject to United Nations approval. The plan was rejected by both Arab and Jewish representatives. In September 1948, Bernadotte was assassinated by a member of the Stern Group. Ben Gurion immediately ordered the arrest of more than 250 members of the Stern Group, and its leaders were imprisoned. The government also ordered the dissolution of the Irgun and the transfer of its members and weapons to the Israel Defence Forces.

On 15 October 1948 the Egyptians cut off Israeli supplies to the Negev - the southern desert area - and war recommenced. Israel took Beersheba and advanced into the Sinai Desert. Heavy fighting in Jerusalem ended with the city divided.

On 7th January 1949 a final cease-fire was called.

The war was now over, and Israel had lost some 6,000 killed, including 4,000 soldiers and 2,000 civilians. Figures for Arab casualties are not readily available.

CONSEQUENCES OF THE WAR for ISRAEL and THE PALESTINIANS to 1967

The Armistice Agreements

After the cease-fire, negotiations took place between Israel and Egypt on the Greek island of Rhodes under the mediation of the American diplomat Ralph Bunche. This led to an armistice agreement which was followed by subsequent agreements with Lebanon, Transjordan and

Syria. The net result of the agreements was the establishment of the cease-fire lines of 1949.

Although the Gaza Strip came under Egyptian control, it was not annexed by Egypt, and its inhabitants were defined as stateless. Syria advanced its boundary from the international boundary, which had been agreed upon by Britain and France in 1923 when Britain transferred the Golan Heights to the French mandate of Syria, to the eastern shore of the Sea of Galilee. Israel expanded its borders beyond the boundaries fixed by the Partition Resolution to include a corridor between Tel Aviv and Jerusalem, the whole of Upper Galilee in the north, and Beersheba in the southern desert.

Note: The agreements at Rhodes were cease-fire agreements only. No Arab country recognized the legitimacy of Israel, and the Arab League still considered its members to be engaged in a continuing war.

Effect on the Palestinians

1. An Arab exodus from the territory which became Israel, took place during the war. That exodus began after the UN Partition Resolution of November 1947, and continued after the date of Israel's Declaration of Independence in May 1948, when the Arab armies invaded.

2. Some hundreds of thousands of Arabs left their homes in the areas which came under Jewish control. Estimates of the number of refugees who left their homes in Israel from 1947 to 1949 vary from 419,000, calculated on the basis of numbers before and after the exodus, to 726,000, based on UNRWA (United Nations Relief and Works Agency) relief figures.

3. Jordan gave refugees citizenship and full rights. Lebanon refused both citizenship and equal rights. Egypt denied refugees in Gaza the right to enter Egypt.

4. The causes of the Arab exodus are the subject of controversy, since the events took place in the heat of war, and most of the reports are politically motivated.

Arab sources accuse the Jewish forces of a concerted terror campaign aimed at removing the Arab population. An Israeli response is to point to the documented Arab calls for the inhabitants of the area to leave their homes and make way for an Arab invasion, and a serious effort by Israel to persuade the Arab population to remain.

Both descriptions of the events probably have an element of truth, depending on the exigencies of full-scale war. For example, the Jewish leadership in the mixed city of Haifa made a point of attempting to persuade the Arab population to remain in place, a call which was resolutely rejected in order to clear the way for the expected invasion of the city. On the other hand some of those who occupied strategically critical areas in the centre of the country between Tel Aviv and Jerusalem were displaced and others fled as a consequence of the highly coloured reports in the Arab media.

Essentially, however, the Arab exodus was result of the fact that the war of 1947-1949 took place, in the sense that if there had been no invasion and a peaceful partition had been completed then it is unlikely that any substantial emigration would have occurred.

5. The Arabs who remained in Israel became Israeli citizens with equal voting rights. However the areas where most of the Arab population lived were placed under military government under the Defence (Emergency) Regulations introduced by the British Mandatory authority, and the freedom of movement of the inhabitants was limited by a requirement for military permission. The restrictions were generally allowed to lapse in the 1960's, and the military government was formally abolished in 1972. There were 11 Arab members elected to the Israeli Parliament in 2006, and an Arab Justice served on the Full Bench of Israel's Supreme Court.

6. The Palestinians who lived in the region outside the 1949 Armistice lines came under the rule of Jordan and Egypt. Those who lived in the area described by the Jordanians as the "West Bank" of the River Jordan, were absorbed into Jordan as Jordanian citizens, although many remained in refugee camps receiving UNRWA aid. Those who lived in Gaza came under Egyptian rule, but did not receive citizenship. Gaza

was not annexed by Egypt and its inhabitants became stateless and were not allowed to enter Egypt without express permission.

Effect on Israel

One of the first Laws of the State of Israel was the "Law of Return", which provided that every Jew was entitled to immigrate to Israel as of right.

Between 15 May 1948 and 31 December 1951 a total of 686,739 Jewish immigrants arrived in Israel. The Jewish population thus grew from about 650,000 in 1948 to about 1.4 million in 1951, causing immense strains on Israel's undeveloped economy, with severe housing and food shortages. The first wave of immigration following independence consisted of over 120,000 survivors of the Nazi holocaust, arriving from the Displaced Persons camps of Europe and the British detention camps in Cyprus. The Romanian government was bribed to permit another 117,950 survivors to leave, and others arrived from Bulgaria and Yugoslavia.

In addition many of the Jewish communities in Arab countries were subjected to active persecution following the creation of Israel. In 1950 the Iraqi government agreed to release its Jews provided they left behind their property and valuables, and a total of 123,371 immigrants were immediately airlifted to Israel. Then followed the arrival of more than 250,000 immigrants from Morocco, 56,000 from Tunisia, 35,000 from Libya, nearly 30,000 from Egypt and 46,640 Jews airlifted from Yemen. In all between 1948 and 1972 about 840,000 Jewish refugees fled from the countries of the Arab world, and about 580,000 found refuge in Israel.

By the mid-1950s the Jewish population was roughly half of European background and half non-European. The vast tent camps were being replaced by permanent housing, and development towns were being established to absorb many of the new immigrants.

The preceding articles offer extremist views but demonstrate the attitudes and relations of the people involved and obviously there are others who see an opportunity to gain something from this. What is striking is Israel's overbearing, cold and clinical attitude to their takeover of somebody else's land, the basic assumption that the land is theirs. Would they have been so cocksure without the backing of the United States? I wonder. One of the Ten Commandments – Thou shalt not covet thy neighbour's land etc. etc. comes to mind.

I find the whole issue absolutely barbaric and the extent of the violence has in no way diminished, in fact with today's technology applied to weapons the disastrous results are greatly multiplied.

"Confusion about the origins of the conflict all too often has obscured Americans' understanding of its true dimension. It began as a conflict resulting from immigrants struggling to displace the local majority population. All else is derivative from this basic reality."

– Donald Neff, former Senior Editor, Time Magazine, Fallen Pillars: U.S. Policy towards Palestine and Israel since 1945

Difficult to not get drawn into taking sides isn't it?

Come back to us God, all is forgiven. I did not want to end the story on such a dismal note but the evidence is there for all to see – from beginning to end of this book – actually a real eye opener for me – is the violence associated with religion. Not just violence per se but it appears to have been a very welcome outlet and reason to resort to baser instincts for some. The very people we should be looking up to for spiritual guidance are the instigators and propagators of absolute misery for innocent people and all because of this phenomenon called 'religion'. It really is politics and aggression in the name of religion.

A figure shown in some documentation is 33,000 plus, this is the number of sects "scattered" around the world. I think this is okay as long as it's a 'live and let live' arrangement with each sect allowing its members freedom of speech and choice and sect leaders offering explanation to members why that particular route was chosen. It's all very well for parents wanting their children to follow them in their choice of religion or church but children, on reaching an age of understanding should also be allowed and encouraged to follow their own path without duress.

I have mentioned all the lives lost because of religion and the argument against that is – but look at all the souls saved – I defy anybody to name one. Despite all the negatives, I have enjoyed the research and I really did have an open mind at the beginning but now I am even more confused and it's not just old age creeping on.

Thanks.

Book List

This list comprises the main books that I consulted and found helpful in consolidating my ramblings and putting them in some sort of order.

Halliday, F. (2005), *100 myths about the Middle East,* London, UK: Saqi Books

Magnussun, M. (1977), *Archaeology of the Bible,* New York: Simon & Schuster

National Geographic. (2006), *History and Faith Cradle&Crucible in the Middle East,* Washington

Nelson-Pallmeyer, J. 2003), *Is Religion Killing Us?* USA: Trinity Press International

Reader's Digest. (1988), *Mysteries of the Bible,* USA

The Holy Bible

The New American Standard Bible

Wilson, T. *Through the Bible,* London: Virtue & Co. Ltd. William Collins & Sons

Blake, D. L. (2008), *A visual History of the English Bible,* Grand Rapids, MI: Baker Books

Avi-Yonath, M. (2001 edition)) *A History of Israel and the Holy Land, The Continuum*

Wade, N. (2009), *The Faith Instinct,* Penguin Books

Peters, F.E. (2003), *The Monotheists,* University Press

Phillips, C. & Axelrod, A. *Encyclopedia of Wars,*

Cahill, T. (1998), *The Gifts of the Jews*, New York: Doubleday

TheReligionofPeace.com

ACKNOWLEDGEMENTS AND CONTRIBUTORS

Thanks are due to the following for permission to reproduce certain passages and maps:

Nicholas Wade, *'The Faith Instinct'* Penguin Books 2009 see Introduction, Religious Thoughts.

Jack Nelson-Pallmeyer, *'Is Religion Killing Us'* USA Trinity Press International see Introduction, Religious Thoughts.

Fred Halliday *'100 Myths About the Middle East'*, UK Saqi Books London 2005. University of California Press see Introduction, Chapter 9, 12, 15, Religious Thoughts.

Mark Throntveit, Professor of Hebrew and Old Testament – Commentary on the Exile Period, see Chapter 7, Religious Thoughts.

Religious Facts.com *'What is the Catholic Religion?'* see Chapter 10, Religious Thoughts.

Professor Mark Damen, The University of Phoenix – The Crusades and Medieval Christianity Section 15, see Chapter 12, Religious Thoughts.

Alison Weir *"If America Knew"*, CounterPunch & AntiWar.com see Conclusion, Religious Thoughts.

Professor Rob J. Hyndman *'The Times: A Chronology of the Bible'*, see Timeline Discussion, Religious Thoughts.

TIMELINE DISCUSSION

It became obvious that I am not alone in trying to rationalise and standardise a timeline for the book. Even the Bible contradicts itself because of the number of scribes who were involved in the writing of it and the different time frames when it was written. I have included some of my notes here, as much for my benefit as anything else but they may help others.

The Times of the Patriarchs from 'The Times' by Rob J. Hyndman

The Times from Abraham to Solomon from 'The Times' by Rob J. Hyndman

World History Chart in Accordance With Bible Chronology from Bible Charts and Maps LLC

Shifting Power in the Ancient World p164-165 - Mysteries of the Bible

Timelines taken from various library books – refer to Book List

Rob J Hyndman is an Australian statistician known for his work on forecasting. He is Professor of Statistics at Monash University and Editor-in-Chief of the International Journal of Forecasting. Wikipedia His website is robjhyndman.com

Born: May 2, 1967, Melbourne

Education: University of Melbourne

1. Introduction from 'The Times: A Chronology of the Bible' by Rob. J.Hyndman (in part). Reprinted with permission.

Knowing about biblical chronology can help us understand why God said what he did and did what he did at each particular time. Sometimes it can also help us understand the relationship of Bible events to other historical events. It is often crucial in determining when a particular prophecy was fulfilled. In short, any serious Bible student needs a good chronology.

The scriptures contain a large amount of chronological information. Some periods of time such as the times of the captivity and the life of Jesus are crucial in biblical history and are recorded in a great deal of detail. For other periods, such as the time between the Testaments, the Bible gives virtually no information. The purpose of this chronology is to piece together the scriptural information, using archaeological and historical data where necessary, to establish the dates and sequence of events in the Bible. The whole of scripture is given some attention, although some periods are presented in more detail than others depending on the quantity of available data.

Absolute dates

In most ancient records (including the Bible), a local event such as the year of a king's accession or a major natural disaster was the common reference point for dating. Using this contemporary information, it is relatively easy to give a correct sequence of events over a short period of time. However, it is much more difficult to establish dates in the modern format using AD and BC dates.

In order to establish these 'absolute' dates, it is often necessary to resort to archaeological research. Babylonian tablets, Egyptian papyri and other contemporary records provide lists of kings, major events in each year and cross checks with contemporary monarchs. In particular, some major astronomical events such as eclipses were noted. Thus, reliable dates of Near Eastern history from about 2000 BC are available. From about 1400 BC, these dates can be established to within a decade. From about 1100 BC, dates can be estimated increasingly accurately with more contemporary information available. The Canon of Ptolemy provides an accurate framework from 620 BC and dates from that point are known often within a few weeks and even to the very day.

Much of this information has only been discovered in the past 100 years, so that Bible chronology is now much better understood than previously. Using the extra-biblical information to fill in the holes in the biblical information, we can construct a fairly accurate chronology from Abraham to Jesus.

This chronology presents almost all dates in the modern Western format as most readers are unfamiliar with other calendars. That is, dates are quoted as BC or AD and the Gregorian calendar is used. The one exception to this is the last week of Jesus' ministry where the Jewish calendar has been used. Without the Jewish calendar, many aspects of the wonderful allegory of Jesus as the Passover lamb would be missed.

Problems

There are a number of notable complications that are often overlooked when establishing a chronology of the Bible. Some events recorded in scripture are concurrent rather than consecutive. For instance the kings of Israel and Judah often reigned with their sons for a period of time. These co-regencies are not explicitly detailed in scripture.

Also, different calendar systems were used by different nations. For example, the Egyptians counted the time between a king's accession and the next New Year's day as his first year, while the Mesopotamians began counting the years of a king's reign from his first New Year's day in office. It appears that Judah usually (but not always) used the Mesopotamian system while Israel used the Egyptian method at first and changed to the Mesopotamian method in about 800 BC. Another calendar problem is the fact that two different calendars were in use in Israel and Judah — one used for religious purposes, the other for secular purposes. The civil calendar began in the month Tishri while the religious calendar began in Nisan. It is not always clear which calendar is being used when the Bible gives a date.

Finally, there is uncertainty in some of the figures. For example, the Septuagint gives several numbers that are quite different from the Masoretic text.

These facts must be considered when attempting to produce an accurate chronology of scripture.

Archaeological references to Israel

The first apparent reference to the children of Israel in secular history occurs in The Armana Letters (1400 BC), discovered in 1887 by an Egyptian peasant woman. They contain a request from the governor of Jerusalem to the Pharaoh of Egypt to help supply military aid against the Habiru people. Many scholars think that this is a reference to the Hebrew invasion of Canaan.

The only other known reference to Israel before the time of the kings is in the Stele of Merneptah (1220 BC). There, Merneptah, Pharaoh of Egypt (1236-1223 BC), mentions that "Israel is laid waste, his seed is not;" apparently referring to an Egyptian victory over Israel during the time of the Judges.

This is the end of Rob.J.Hyndman excerpts.

The World History Chart in Accordance with Bible Chronology from Bible Charts and Maps LLC

This timeline uses the Masoretic Text and lists Ussher's Table. Also a tremendous amount of World History is listed.

Other 'chronology' authors – Louis Ginzberg

J. Finegan – Handbook of Biblical Chronology

James Ussher – 17th Cent Bishop 4004BC – date of creation

Dr. R. C. Wetzel

Calendars: Gregorian, Egyptian, Jewish, Israel & Judah religious, Israel & Judah secular,

Mesopotamian method,

Septuagint text, Masoretic text, Samaritan text

Ussher method

The Gregorian Calendar also known as the Western or Christian calendar is the internationally accepted and the most widely used civil calendar.

The Julian calendar results in a shortened drift of about three days every 400 years.

The Egyptian calendar is 365 days long.

The Jewish calendar is predominantly used for religious observances eg. the current year of the Jewish calendar 16 September 2012 to 4 September 2013 is 5773.

Mesopotamian method used for agricultural purposes based on seasons and lunar cycles.

The Septuagint or Greek Old Testament is an ancient translation of the Hebrew Bible. It is quoted in the New Testament and continues to serve as the Eastern Orthodox Old Testament. Masoretic text is the authoritative Hebrew text of the Jewish Bible and is also widely uses as the basis for translations of the Old Testament in Protestant Bibles and also recently for some Catholic Bibles although the Eastern Orthodox continue to use Septuagint as they hold it divinely inspired.

Samaritan Pentateuch also called Samaritan Torah is a version of the Hebrew language Pentateuch, the first five books of the Bible, traditionally written in the Samaritan alphabet and used by the Samaritans.

Ussher method – basically the proposed date of Creation is 4004BC.

Louis Ginzberg -

Rabbi **Louis Ginzberg** was a Talmudist and leading figure in the Conservative Movement of Judaism of the twentieth century. He was born on November 28, 1873, in Kaunas, Vilna Governorate; he died on November 11, 1953, in New York City.

J. Finegan - **Jack Finegan** (1908-2000)[1] was an American biblical scholar. He was notable for his views on biblical chronology.[2] "Handbook of Biblical Chronology" too complex for me.

James Ussher - **James Ussher** (sometimes spelled *Usher*, 4 January 1581 – 21 March 1656) was Church of Ireland Archbishop of Armagh and Primate of All Ireland between 1625 and 1656. He was a prolific scholar, who most famously published a chronology that purported to establish the time and date of the creation as the night preceding Sunday, 23 October 4004 BC, according to the proleptic Julian calendar

Dr.R.C.Wetzel – Baptist Pastor

4004 Archbishop JAMES USSHER'S 1654 date of the Creation of Man.

3975 FRANK KLASSEN'S 1975 date of the Creation of Man.

3845 SETH was born to ADAM.

3760 Traditional Jewish date of the Creation of Man

So there we are, my Timeline ramblings.

My idea of a timeline was to have a base, in my case this was to be 'actual historical events', which have been confirmed or verified and accepted, then, corresponding to the time of these actual historical events, other happenings, specifically Biblical or Religious in context. My notes (not included), show an attempt to do this and also demonstrate the complex time difference in the Bible itself.

I have decided that it is futile and a waste of time to try and reconcile these time differences but where the Bible and archaeological evidence conflict I have no hesitation in accepting the archaeological evidence. I have used the World History Chart as published by Bible Charts and Maps LLC as a guide where there is no other information in my notes.

Rather than get bogged down trying to establish sensible dates I will try and concentrate on the theme of the book which is:

Religion - What may be considered to be, not just its negative and violent impact on the world to date but also to try and understand why there are so many 'religions'. Why were they formed? Or are they just derivatives or sects of the original?

The content and title of the chapters will forego the inclusion of a separate TimeLine section.

CPSIA information can be obtained at www.ICGtesting.com
Printed in the USA
LVOW13s0519090714

393433LV00001B/6/P